NO GREATER LOVE

WORLD WAR ONE REMEMBERED

Angus H Shaw

All profits from the sale of this book go to Poppy Scotland

First published in the United Kingdom by Angus H Shaw in 2018

Paradise, Craigrothie, Cupar, Fife KY15 5PH

shawangus3@gmail.com

ISBN 978-0-9954887-2-4

A catalogue record for this book is available from the British Library.

Cover picture drawn by Helen Paterson
Copy Editing and Layout Angus H Shaw

DEDICATED TO ALL WHO HAVE GIVEN THEIR LIVES FOR OTHERS

"Greater love hath no man than this,
that a man lay down his life for his friends"

John 15:13

Contents

ILLUSTRATION CREDITS

Acknowledgements

This volume is largely a compilation of material that has been made available to me. Without the generous contributions it would not have been possible to bring this together. Those who provided material include Clara Brunton, Jane Buchanan; Jean Finlay; Elder Garland; Jan Howie; Eckard Lange; Scott (Old Man) McAuly of Melrose, Massachusetts; Wilma Nicol; Helen Paterson; Ann Shaw; Alexander Smillie; Margaret Sproule. I particularly wish to thank Robert Carmichael for translating documents from German in the Fraktur script into English. I also wish to thank my wife Ann for taking time to proof read this book before it went to the printer. She, along with others not named, has given valued support in this venture.

Introduction

I t is the purpose of this book to consider the human cost of World War One. While emphasis has been given to the German, British and American conflict there is no intention to demean the contribution of all those people around the world who bravely sacrificed themselves in the tragedy that was World War One.

Here you will find examples of the courage, bravery and nobility of men and women who fought and others who stayed at home because they believed it was right. Motivation came through faith in God, loyalty to the monarch and love of friends and family. Political ineptitude led to the events that resulted in this conflict. Those at the front and those at home showed tremendous bravery and courage in enduring the grave hardships of the time. There were those who endured the shells, the fear and the horror of the trenches. There were also those at home who suffered, worried and wept.

There is a strong desire to dehumanise the enemy during a war. It is easier to kill a brute or an animal than to kill another who is like yourself. With the benefit of hindsight and the loyalty of friendships across international borders, hated enemies of 100 years ago are now our friends.

In the words of the composer Karl Jenkins:

Better is peace than always war
And better is peace than evermore war
Always war, always war
Better is peace than evermore war
And better and better is peace
(From: The Armed Man: A Mass for Peace)

CHAPTER 1

WHY WAR?

Why did Europe, "bursting with health and abundance," fall into "a rage of self-mutilation that could not but sap its strength for a century or more, and perhaps forever"?
Aleksandr Solzhenitsyn (1983 Templeton Prize Lecture)

There are those who claim that the 20th century did not start until August 4th 1914. All other major events throughout that century are consequential upon World War One. The German/ Austro-Hungarian, Ottoman and Russian empires collapsed. The United States emerged as leader of the Western powers. Russia was overtaken by communism which led to the emergence of the Cold War after 1945. The failure of the Treaty of Versailles to establish a stable Europe resulting in the rise of Nazism, the Wall Street crash and World War II, all followed the end of the War to end Wars! Indeed it has been claimed that the effects of WWI did not reach a conclusion until the fall of the Soviet Union in 1991. That conclusion ignores the importance of the development of the European Union which has brought political stability in Europe and grown in influence on the world stage throughout the latter half of the 20th century and into the 21st. Through this organisation Germany has come to dominate Europe both politically and economically. In 1914 many believed the war was necessary to prevent such an occurrence but then history follows its own course and the world is a very different place from what it was in 1914.

The War also changed society with the emergence of women in the work place and the momentum this gave to the cause of feminism. Financial hardship, resulting from the cost of war, meant that there was little economic growth throughout the first half of the 1900s. Certainly the living conditions of many in 1950 Scotland were not very different from those of 1910. Small tenement houses with outside toilet and often also an outside tap remained in many towns and villages. There was a considerable number of people who depended upon gas or paraffin for lighting as electricity was not available for them until well into the 1950s. This lack of development was a result of the financial commitment our country entered into in order to participate in the carnage that was the First and later the Second World War.

It was on page six that the Scotsman of August 5th 1914 intimated: "It was officially announced in London ten minutes after midnight that owing to the summary rejection by the German Government of the request made by His Majesty's Government for assurance that the neutrality of Belgium will be respected, His Majesty's Ambassador at Berlin has received his passport. His Majesty's government has declared to the German Government that a state of war exists between Great Britain and Germany as from 11 p.m. on August 4."

Positioned as it was beneath the intimation of the rising and falling of the sun and moon, with no head-line above it, there seems to have been little effort to emphasise the significance of the event. To be fair, while this is the first mention of the declaration of War in the Scotsman on that day it is given greater significance elsewhere in that edition.

Although there are several identifiable political situations that led to war, it is hard to establish the reasons for the outbreak of hostilities. The series of crises appears to have started on June 28th 1914 with the assassination of Archduke Franz Ferdinand, heir to the Austrian throne and his wife Sophie, Duchess of Hohenberg, when on a visit to Sarajevo. Austria believed the assassination to have been initiated by the Serbian Nationalist Movement. On July 23rd Austria-Hungary, with German support, delivered an ultimatum to Serbia. The Serbs spoke of arbitration but began to mobilise their army. Two days later Austria – Hungary broke diplomatic relations with Serbia and mobilised its army. On July 26th Britain tried to convene a conference of major European countries to resolve the situation. While France, Italy and Russia agreed to take part, Germany did not. On July 30th Austria started shelling Belgrade, the capital of Serbia and the following day Russia began full mobilisation in support of their old friends. Germany demanded that Russia cease its preparations for war and its refusal lead to the German declaration of war against Russia on the first day of August. Believing that France would support Russia, Germany decided that if it, the weaker of the two, was taken out of the conflict, Germany could concentrate its efforts on the Eastern front. In fact France had made no effort to mobilise its troops but Germany claimed it had bombed Nuremberg and so said that the Fatherland was in danger.

On August 3rd Germany declared war on France and invaded neutral Belgium which it saw as a route through which it could attack France. Britain demanded that Germany retreat from Belgium. This was ignored and so on August 4th Britain declared war on Germany. These were the days of the British Empire and so Britain's declaration involved Canada, Australia, New Zealand, India and South Africa. On August 6th Austria-Hungary declared war on Russia. So Europe and the countries of the British Empire were at war.

It appears there was no reason for the war taking place for, at any stage, the situation could have been deflated by talks, and disagreements settled. The political situation in Europe was complicated with the unification of Germany and the development of a power struggle between two major European power blocks that started at the end of the 19th century. Germany, Austria-Hungary and Italy formed the Triple Alliance while Britain, Russia and France formed the Triple Entente.

Errors made by the political leaders escalated the rhetoric and this resulted in the mobilisation of forces. There was also, amongst some, the development of a mindset that a war could be useful and people quickly started talking of when there will be war rather than if there will be war. Another factor is that while in Britain it was the Cabinet that had to approve the declaration of war, in Russia and Germany the Czar and the Kaiser had sole authority to make that decision. Perhaps they were not the best people to hold such power.

The French believed they were defending their country against Germany which they saw as an aggressive foe. There had been ill feeling between France and Germany ever since the latter annexed Alsace-Lorraine in the 1870s. The average British soldier wasn't too clear why he was involved: hence the popular ditty of the time, "We're Here Because We're Here". At the beginning of the war the Germans believed they were defending Germany against an aggressive alliance of nations that was out to destroy their country. In 1916 they believed they were not only defending Germany but also French civilians who were caught up in the British assault. Many villages were destroyed by British shells and the Germans took the people to safety and rebuilt their villages. In the Battle of the Somme the British were seen to have launched a massive attack on the 'Fatherland' and the Germans believed they were protecting their country against an invader. Most Germans continued to think of the war in this way and so they refused to accept article 231 of the Treaty of Versailles that Germany was guilty of being the aggressor.

So why did World War One start? The Cambridge historian Christopher Clerk points out that the story of the cause of the war is centred upon a series of myths that were seen as undeniable truths. So it is that Austria believed it was threatened by Serbia and Serbia believed it was a victim of suppression by the Austro-Hungarian Empire. Germany believed it had cause to fear invasion while Russia believed it was being humiliated by its powerful neighbours. France believed it was in danger of being dominated by a more powerful Germany while Britain believed it was in everyone's interests to ensure that no one power would dominate Europe. The USA had no interest in European politics while Japan had designs on the domination of Asia. The paranoia that abounded around the world was dangerous. If statesmen are foolish enough to believe such narratives then the world is in peril.

The fact is that poor decisions were being made by all participants across Europe including Britain. Laying blame on any one nation is difficult for all played their part. On July 28th Churchill wrote to his wife Clementine saying a "wave of madness ... has swept the mind of Christendom". Two days later the German Chief of Staff Moltke warned his government that, "the civilised states of Europe will begin to tear one another to pieces" in a conflict that would "annihilate the civilisation of almost the whole of Europe for decades to come." It was the stories of dangers and threats that they all believed that made them feel war was necessary and inevitable.

By the end of 1914 it was clear that the war would not be 'over by Christmas', as predicted by the popular press. Already the war had reached a stalemate with the two sides pounding one another in what was the greatest European blood-letting in history.

Owen Chadwick, in the 1973-74 Gifford Lectures said that in the 19th century there was a "secularization of the European mind". This, he claims, played its part in creating the conditions in the political mind that diminished any restraint or set of moral rules in the way the war was conducted. The attack on Biblical theology as expressed by such 19th century thinkers as Marx and Nietzsche replaced the God-centred faith of European churches with a god of national identity. The God of the Bible became the god of my country and the reason for my country's moral superiority. Inevitably this led to the dehumanising of other races. As Aleksandr Solzhenitsyn said later, it was because "Men had forgotten God".

As the war dragged on more and more German soldiers of all ranks began to call for a compromise peace which accepted the position as it stood at that time. They wanted to denounce the high ranking officers who sought to prolong the war to achieve victory through one decisive battle. It was becoming increasingly obvious that this was not going to happen. Attacks at Verdun and The Somme led to a war of attrition that was impossible to win. By the summer of 1918 the German army was disillusioned; many knowing the war could not be won. It has been suggested they were war-weary and consequently less effective as a fighting force.

On November 12th 1918, the day after the Treaty of Versailles was signed, Hindenburg announced, "You have kept the enemy from crossing our frontiers and you have saved your country from the miseries and disasters of war. We end the struggle proudly and with our heads held high where we have stood for four years in the face of a world full of enemies." The German army felt stabbed in the back by their politicians. The sense of betrayal was reinforced by the terms of the treaty of Versailles which led to the economic destruction of Germany in the 1920s.

Whatever the truth or falsehood of the reasons for the war, it is clear that the ordinary German soldier believed he was doing exactly what the British, French and allied soldiers believed they were doing; protecting their country against an aggressive foe. On all sides ordinary people were fed with the propaganda that the political elite wanted them to believe. It was the ordinary people and not the political elite that had to go out to the front line and pay the price in mud and blood for the consequences of political ineptitude. On both sides noble men were fighting for noble reasons and dying in their millions.

No doubt others would view the situation differently but to me the countries of Europe were behaving like children in a playground goading one another to take action. Action was indeed taken to devastating effect. Many historians find it hard to find any justification for the outbreak of hostilities in 1914 which eventually involved the whole world.

So began the bloodiest war in the history of the world. It is popular to believe that no one knew what sort of war it would be when it started in 1914. Yet, on August 5th the Aberdeen

Evening Express contained a recruitment advertisement under the Royal Coat of Arms which declared: "Your King and Country need you. Will you answer your Country's Call? Each day is fraught with the gravest possibilities, and at this very moment the Empire is on the brink of the greatest war in the history of the world." Clearly the political leaders were aware of the potential of the coming conflict to be utterly devastating. It is also clear that the public was not being protected from this belief. Nevertheless, in August 1914 the man and woman in the street saw the war as a bit of excitement and anyway, "It would all be over by Christmas"!

American Catholic theologian George Weigel, senior fellow of the Ethics and Public Policy Centre, in the William E. Simon Lecture which he delivered in 2014 explained the cause of World War I this way:

"The European world that went to war in 1914—the world that may yet prove to have bled itself of civilisational vitality in the Great War—was one in which the masters of the world's leading civilization believed they could create a humane future without the God of the Bible. What they proved, however, was that they could only build a world against each other, which was a world with no future."

The Drama Unfolds

While it is hard to get precise figures for the number of soldiers killed during the war, it has been estimated that of the 60,000,000 soldiers (on all sides) who fought in World War One, 9,000,000, or 14%, died. That amounted to 6,000 each day. In addition there were in the region of 7,000,000 civilians killed. The world had never seen such slaughter. We will never know exactly what the death toll was for so many went missing and others died years later of injuries sustained in the war. While combat killed a large number, disease also exerted a heavy toll, particularly amongst the Turkish troops who were not inoculated against infection. These figures are not impersonal statistics. Each number was a person – a son, father, brother, friend.

Perhaps your grandfather, great uncle or distant cousin was one of these people. We must remember that each number signified the loss of a life and each life was precious. On August 5th 1914 none of this had happened and the tragedy that was about to unfold was hidden from eager young recruits to the armed forces.

It is the intention of this anthology of memories to look at the people, whether allied to Britain or to Germany and remember their sacrifice in an evil of great magnitude that was not of their making.

It is worth remembering that one of the greatest weapons in the armoury of all warring governments is propaganda. Through the spread of misinformation the enemy is de-humanised. They become the embodiment of evil. This makes it easier to attack, maim and kill them. To the British the Germans were 'The Hun' and the soldier was 'Fritz'. To the Germans the British were 'Inselaffe' or Island Monkeys' and the soldier 'Tommy'. In the game of war one side is no better or worse than the other. As the saying goes, "All is fair in love and war!" Or is it?

CHAPTER 2

Who Went To War?

Forgotten Heroes

In Europe in 1916 labourers were becoming increasingly scarce due to the high casualty rate at the Front. In order to address this shortfall a recruitment campaign took place in China. The 96,000 Chinese farm labourers who left their homes in 1916 to assist Britain and her allies to defeat Germany became the forgotten heroes of World War One.

Many of these simple folk thought that on arrival at Shanghai they had reached Europe. In fact, they had only started on a journey that many would not complete. First there was a voyage over the Pacific Ocean which was followed by a six day journey crossing Canada in a sealed train. The reason for sealing the train was to avoid paying taxes. It was then on by ship to Liverpool, train to Folkestone and so to France and Belgium. Those who died on the voyage were buried in Liverpool.

Once at their destination they stayed in labour camps and were given work digging trenches, building roads, repairing tanks, laying railway tracks and unloading ships and trains. They had to work 10 hour days for seven days each week. Three days of annual leave was granted including Chinese New Year. The Chinese labour corps worked alongside the British, Indian, Australian and Canadian soldiers digging the trenches on the Western Front. They were engaged by both the French and the British to do this hard and laborious task. After the signing of the

Armistice in 1918 the allied forces returned home. The Chinese labourers had to remain. Their task was to clear the battlefields of spent and live weaponry and exhume bodies from battlefield graves moving them to the new designated war cemeteries. Their service to the allies did not end until 1920.

Much of the work was carried out within the firing line. While 2,000 Chinese men are buried in official graves, it is believed that as many as 20,000 lost their lives. In return the British gave them a bronze medal to recognize their service; unlike the silver medals British soldiers received it bore only their numbers and not their names. A victory painting now displayed in Paris and started in 1914 aimed to represent all nationalities who, it was hoped, would participate in the victory over Germany. When the United States joined the war in 1917 room had to be made to represent them. In order to do this the Chinese were painted out. Over the years the valuable contribution of these people has been ignored. When the Imperial War Museum was reopened at a cost of £40,000,000 it maintained the silence on the Chinese involvement in the War. Thanks to the efforts of the Chinese community in Britain a new, permanent memorial is being built in London and due to be unveiled in August 2018. This recognition of the sacrifice of the 96,000 is long overdue.

China entered the war in 1917 when a German submarine sank the French ship Athos, killing 543 Chinese people.

The Empire

In 1914 Britain lacked the military resources to wage war in Europe without the support of the Empire. The response from the 'Colonies and Dominions' was overwhelming. France and Britain between them had colonies that stretched across Africa. Canada, Australia and New Zealand gave willing help as did India with its impressive Ghurkha Regiments. It is estimated that about 4 million non-white troops participated in the war. This number includes U.S. soldiers. There were 1.5 million Indian soldiers who fought both in Europe and Asia, 16,000 from the West Indies, 15,000 from the Caribbean. In addition there were French colonial troops from West Africa, Indochina, North African countries and so the list goes on and on. There is no doubt that this quickly became a war of global significance.

In Britain we tend to see it as a European war. Americans, too, see it this way and have been known to refer to it as "The European War". In fact, with the declaration of War in August 1914, many overseas territories suddenly found themselves at war with their neighbours; export of cocoa from the Gold Coast to Germany stopped and the transport of goods to the U.K. became more difficult due to the German policy to isolate Britain and so the price of their goods fell dramatically.

First World War memories of such countries as Sri Lanka, India, Namibia, Kenya, Iraq and Egypt are very different from those of Britain, France and Germany. Japan sided with Britain and assisted India in the capture of German territory of Tsangtau on the Chinese coast. South African forces under the leadership of General Smuts invaded German South West Africa. On the other hand Trinidad gained financially because its oil reserves suddenly became important in the war effort.

An unexpected consequence of the war on the peoples of the Dominions was a rise in a sense of nationhood. There was the promise of political independence to Jews and Arabs and greater autonomy for India had the same effect.

By the end of the war the dead belonged to the global community with, for example, about 17,000,000 Indians and about a quarter of the population of Samoa losing their lives.

At the end of the war there were expressions of gratitude to "Dominions of Canada, Australia, New Zealand and South Africa, and our Indian Empire" and of their gratitude for the "unsolicited, help of the Mother Country". Perhaps this statement reflected more upon the British Imperial view of the war than that of the Colonies and Dominions.

The Boys Who Joined Up

According to official government policy, no one could join up to serve their country if they were under the age of 18 and so could not be sent to fight until they were 19. In fact about 250,000 boys under the age of 18 served in the British Army during World War I. Reasons for boys joining up varied. Some sought adventure while others wanted to escape the harshness of life at home. Many were gripped by a nationalistic fervour and wanted to do their bit in the service of King and country. The Recruitment officers clearly knew that the boys were under age, but that did not prevent them from signing up the young lads. Perhaps the two shillings and six pence (12.5p) for each new recruit influenced their decision or perhaps they thought the food and army life would do them good. The 'medical' ensured that the recruit was fit enough, not whether he was old enough. Society as a whole seemed to encourage these young lads to sign up in the army with teachers, parents and even MPs supporting them.

One 15 year old from Cornwall, Cyril Jose, lived in an area of high unemployment. He was also seeking adventure. On one occasion when writing to his sister he boasted about having his own rifle and 2ft long bayonet. By the end of the war his experiences in France made him a life long opponent of militarism.

There was the 17 year old who had been wounded in 1915. The boy was suffering from what was known as 'shock'. He was still unwell when sent back to the front in 1916. Again he was under heavy attack and found himself wandering in a dazed state along the British lines. He was arrested, charged with desertion and shot.

Sixteen year old St John Battersby was a Lieutenant with responsibilities far beyond his age. In spite of being wounded he returned to France where his leg was blown off. After the war he became an English country Vicar. His son tells that his experiences in the war were with him on his death bed when he was shouting, "The Bosch are coming. We're going over the top now"! Clearly this man carried a great burden throughout his life.

One man remembering Passchendaele recalled 'going over the top' in the following words: "It is utterly impossible to describe one's feelings during the hours of waiting for 'zero hour' - the mind is full of wild thoughts and fancies which are utterly beyond control. Recollections of friends and dear ones, places we have seen and known and different phases of life all seem to pass in review before one's eyes and one is recalled to the bitter realities of the moment by the officer's voice: 'Fifteen minutes to go, boys, get ready.'

Immediately there is a great stir and excitement, a final setting of equipment and examination of arms and then a handshake with one or two dear comrades. 6.45 am, 'Over you go, boys,' and we are away on that strange journey across No-Man's Land"

Life In The Trenches

The cheerful young lads who went off to 'do their bit' had no idea what trench warfare was all about. These trenches became the home for the troops as they confronted 'the enemy'. There was nothing glamorous about these deep ditches in which soldiers lived and died. They were dirty, smelly and full of rats and disease. Cholera and trench foot (an infection of the feet caused by prolonged exposure to damp, infection and cold) were a constant fear and lice were the never ending plague. In bad weather it was mud that made life most difficult. During the battle of Passchendaele it rained for three weeks and with up to two feet of water life in the trenches became impossible. The wounded had to get rid of their kilts because the mud on the pleats made them so heavy they couldn't walk in them. Shell holes filled with water and men sank into them and drowned in the filthy stinking mud. Another facet of trench life was exhaustion. One soldier recorded, "The fatigue in that mud was something terrible. It did get to you, and you reached a point where there was no beyond, you just could not go any further. And that's the point I'd reached."

The experiences of the German soldier or Landser were very similar to that of their British or French counterpart. While

German trenches tended to be of superior construction there was still the terrible loss of life; rotting corpses; damp, cold; mud, rats and lice. Everyone who survived this war, German or allied British soldier, was deeply affected for the rest of their lives. Some handled it by becoming tough, some became religious, and many became pacifists. A large number failed to cope at all. These men were first labelled cowards and shot. Later they were diagnosed as hysterical and later still were seen as 'shell shocked'. Today we would say their symptoms suggested 'post traumatic stress disorder' or PTSD.

Women at War
While most of those in the armed forces were men, women served as nurses at the front and many were killed. At home the munitions factories depended almost wholly on women. Many of these factories involved handling poisonous material and it is believed that about 400 women died of exposure to TNT which had severe effects including blood and liver disorders. After the introduction of conscription in 1916, women also found themselves being employed to take over the jobs previously done by men. While expected to do the same work as their men folk, they were not given the same pay. This led to unhappiness and, in 1918, a strike by women on London buses and trams. This was the first example of women taking industrial action to promote equal pay and they won.

Women did not like being excluded from the front line and as a result of pressure the Women's Army Auxiliary Corps (WAAC) was established at the end of 1916. One year later the Women's Royal Naval Service (WRENS) was created and in April 1918 the Women's Royal Air Force was established. As a result of this more than 100,000 women joined Britain's armed forces during the war.

Not all women waited for the formation of the women's services. The Edinburgh doctor Elsie Inglis approached the War Office offering to use her skills in aid of the war. The reply she got was, "My good lady, go home and sit still." Such condescension was not appreciated by the lady responsible for launching the Scottish Women's Suffrage Federation in 1906. Rejection came also from the Red Cross and the Royal Army Medical Corps. Elsie decided that if anything was going to be done she would have to do it herself. As a result of her determination she set up the Scottish Women's Hospitals on the fighting front with 17 around Europe and a number of small hospitals and dressing stations. The first of these was the 200 bed Abbaye de Royaumont hospital which was, like the later hospitals, staffed almost entirely by women. This was made possible by the support of the French who saw the value of her work while the British remained negative. In total, during the war, over 1,000 women served as doctors, nurses, drivers and orderlies in her hospitals across Europe.

Dr Elsie Inglis

Elsie went to Serbia early in 1915 where, accompanied by a women's medical unit, she employed her skills tending the sick and wounded. At one point she was captured by the Austrians but pressure from neutral U.S. gained her release. Following this she returned to the UK and started raising funds for a hospital in

Russia. In 1916 she set off to that country and began working with Serbian soldiers who found themselves in Russia having fled the German troops. In 1917 Elsie became ill with cancer and had to return home. She died the day after she arrived in Newcastle and her body was taken to Edinburgh to lie in state in St Giles Cathedral.

The account above is only the last four years of the life of a lady who had a remarkable career not only as a doctor but as a fighter for women's rights. Elsie was only 53 when she died but she left an extraordinary legacy.

One cannot mention the women of World War One without including Edith Cavell. Edith was born in 1865 in a small village near Norwich where her father was the clergyman. In 1896 she began training as a nurse at the Royal Hospital in Whitechapel and on completion of her training in 1898 Edith gained experience in various hospitals. Before long she went to Brussels to nurse a sick child. While there she was invited to be Matron of the first Nursing School in Belgium.

When War broke out Edith was in Norwich but felt she had to return to Belgium where she believed she could put her training to some practical use. It was her belief that she should help the injured whoever they were. This included German and Austrian soldiers. She was heavily criticised for this by the British. Soon, however, she began to work with others to smuggle allied soldiers out of the hospital and across the border to neutral Holland. At this time she is believed to have saved the lives of over 200 men.

The Germans became suspicious of her activities and she, with others, was arrested. She was tried for treason and the punishment was execution by firing squad. So, at dawn on October 12th 1915 Edith was put to death. Her case and her sentence were widely known and many petitions were sent to the German authorities but to no avail. Edith Cavell has become one of the great heroines of World War I, and indeed of the 20th century.

Nurse Edith Cavell

CHAPTER 3

Caring for the Wounded

Among the bravest participants in World War One were the stretcher bearers. They were largely unsung heroes who made it their business to get to the shell craters and provide first aid to the injured and get them back to the hospital as quickly as possible.

In the Faculty of Arts, Humanities & Cultures 2000 Research Project, the University of Leeds records the memories of Chris, a stretcher bearer in World War One. His account tells how he and his friend Edgar would go out with their stretcher and look for the wounded soldiers. He described the stretchers as rubbish being heavy and narrow. As they searched for the wounded they were often under machine gun fire. At times it was necessary to climb down into shell holes to look for casualties. Once found they would be carried back to the dressing station to be tended by a doctor.

The road back through the narrow trenches was hard and the ground was slippery. Chris said the injured always asked the same question "Is it much further?"

Chris was deeply affected by the sight of so many young men killed and hideously wounded. He felt frustrated at his lack of medical knowledge for he desperately wanted to do something for them. Some of the casualties had been lying there for a long time, even days, but somehow managed to survive until they got to the dressing station. There was a terrible shortage of doctors and stretcher bearers but those who were there worked as hard as they could. On one occasion Chris was asked by a doctor to help him. He was told to hold the patient's arm. Quickly the arm was amputated and Chris was left holding it! This patient seemed to suffer no pain when the operation was carried out but Chris found that the badly wounded frequently seemed to feel no pain.

The Dressing Station was the first of a chain of medical centres established to treat the injured. When a major battle raged the number of casualties was enormous. Stretcher bearers were constantly delivering new cases and there was insufficient staff to deal with the numbers. As a result, queues of men on stretchers developed each one in a desperate state and needing urgent care. One account is of an Ambulance driver who was seconded to help the staff in the station. He worked for three days until he was ready to drop. When he eventually stopped for rest there were still sixty or seventy men waiting to be seen.

Next, the men were taken by Field Ambulance to the casualty clearing stations. Some ambulances were motor driven but many were horse drawn wagons. Roads were either in a poor state or non- existent. Each ambulance was packed with as many men as possible and speed was vital for many were bleeding badly, their comfort had to take a lower priority. Those with broken limbs had a very painful journey to the Casualty Clearing Station.

One soldier recalled his experience as a casualty. A piece of shrapnel had penetrated his thigh. At first he thought it was a lump of earth that hit him until he felt the warm blood running down his leg. Eventually he collapsed in a copse where he lay for some time until the stretcher bearers found him and took him to the dressing station. The medics looked exhausted as they went about their duties bringing such relief and comfort as they could to the injured. Next morning he was loaded on to one of the ambulance wagons to be taken to the main Casualty Clearing Station. He said they were, "loaded like loaves of bread into a baker's oven". The horse galloped across the battlefield which was still under fire and inside the wounded had to bear the agony of their wounds as they were tossed around over the rutted road – if there was a road! One man who had abdominal wounds was in intense pain. Each jolt of the wagon felt like the blow of a hammer on his wounds.

He begged his comrades to shoot him as an act of mercy. No one answered his call. That memory came from Ernst Junger, a highly decorated German soldier who became famous for the book, 'Storm of Steel' which records his memoirs as a serving officer in World War One.

Ernst Junger

Many famous people served as Ambulance drivers. These included composers Maurice Ravel and Ralph Vaughan Williams; film maker Walt Disney; writers Ernest Hemingway, Jerome K. Jerome and Somerset Maugham. Not so famous but important to my family is my wife Ann's Grandfather, Fred Mitchell, who, as a staff sergeant, served as an ambulance driver. Though mentioned in despatches (we know not why) he had little to say of his experiences. It was directly as a result of what he saw in World War One that he became a life long conscientious objector. I was privileged to have known Fred before he died in 1982. I found him to be a very kind man with a profound Christian faith who lived by a very clear moral compass. When War broke out again in 1939 he found himself working with the Christian Pacifist Forestry and Land Units to find gainful employment for the new generation of C.Os.

Other notable people of the time such as Fr. Teilhard de Chardin, the French Jesuit priest, theologian and author and Fr

Angelo Giuseppe Roncalli, later Pope John XXIII acted as stretcher bearers while author of Dr. Findlay's Casebook, A. J. Cronin, was a Royal Navy Surgeon.

Fred Mitchell R.A.M.C.

Once at the Casualty Clearing Station the condition of the patient had to be assessed quickly. With loss of blood many men were in a very poor condition when they arrived. The surgeon had to decide quickly whether or not an amputation was required. It would appear that damaged limbs were the most common injuries. One doctor tells how at times he had to work very long hours – 21 hours working, three hours sleep and another twenty one hours working. Nurses too were busy helping with theatre work and also seeing to dressings and the general comfort of their patients. Conditions were poor with tents being used as hospitals. At times operations had to be carried out under candlelight.

Occasionally they would find themselves under attack but mostly they were away from the front line. One recent innovation that saved many lives was the use of blood transfusions. This was used extensively in the Casualty Clearing Stations.

When the men were considered to be in a stable condition they were sent either to a convalescent camp or to a Base Hospital like one at Rouen in France. There they would be placed in wards according to their injuries. Those with brain damage were in one ward, those with abdominal injuries in another and those with leg wounds and amputees in yet another ward. The greatest fear was of gas gangrene for this infection was almost always fatal. These were the days before the development of antibiotics and there was little effective control of infection. Once again the demand for beds was great and it was necessary to move patients on as soon as they were able to make room for new casualties. Nurses were liable to become ill. Working with patients with gas gangrene was especially demanding and they were also open to any infection that was around. Whilst many casualties died during the War, many others survived thanks to the hard work and dedication of nurses, doctors and volunteers.

CHAPTER 4

Those Who stayed at Home

To begin with, volunteers to the armed services were sufficient to meet demand. By 1916 it was clear that more men were needed. In March of that year the government passed the Military Service Act which declared that all medically fit single men between the ages of 18 and 41 were to enlist in the armed forces. In May of the same year married men were included. Later the age limit was raised to 50. Men who were conscripted in to service had no choice which service they would enter, they had to go where it was felt they were most needed.

Men in some occupations were exempt. This included clergymen, teachers, coal miners, and doctors; workers in the iron and steel industry and others in occupations that were seen as important in supporting the war effort. Examples of such occupations included those of my two grandfathers. One was a relief signalman on the railways. This was seen as an important position for the movement of men and supplies around the country. My other grandfather was a marine engineer working on trawlers in Aberdeen. His role was important in securing food for the people at home.

It was possible to apply for exemption due to poor health, potential damage to business, family hardship or conscientious objection (those who believed war and killing was wrong for religious reasons). Those exempt because they worked in what

was known as a 'Scheduled Occupation' were given badges(left) to confirm they were doing their part in war service. This was necessary because of the social pressure that existed amongst the wider population to ensure everyone played their part. Why should one man have to go and put his life at risk to fight in the trenches while another stayed at home?

Conscientious Objectors

The inclusion of conscientious objectors in the United Kingdom to the list of those exempt from compulsory military service was aimed at defusing objections to conscription. After all, this was the first war in which it was considered necessary to introduce compulsory recruitment and politicians were aware that it may not be universally welcomed.

Sixteen thousand men from across Britain are recorded as having been Conscientious Objectors (COs). Compared to the six million who served, this number is small but their impact was considerable. Most COs were pacifist for religious reasons with many being Quakers (The Religious Society of Friends). Others were Christian fundamentalists while still others were politically motivated. A third group were 'Humanists' who believed it was wrong to kill but not for religious reasons. A fourth group simply objected to government interference in their lives.

COs were largely viewed as cowards. They were vilified, abused, forced into the army, brutalised and tortured. Some were even sentenced to death in order to break their resistance. Many spent months or even years in prison. The authorities failed, however, to break their resolve. Those who believed that killing was wrong were resolute and they stand as an example to this day of the importance of individual conscience.

The effect on the family of being a CO was great. Some were abused by neighbours and some families split permanently. This left many COs with a great sense of guilt. Clearly being a CO was not the coward's way out for it took great courage to make such a stand.

In Germany Conscientious Objectors were even worse off than their British counterparts. Unlike Britain, German conscription laws made no provision for conscientious objectors. Most were members of such religious organisations as Jehovah Witnesses, Mennonites and Seventh Day Adventists. If members of these groups agreed to enlist they were given non-combative duties. This was an unofficial arrangement. Anyone who refused to enlist or take any part in the war was considered to be either mad or guilty of desertion. As a result these people spent the war either in a mental hospital or in prison. In this way such 'trouble makers' were kept out of the way and given no platform from which to spread their views.

Ernst Friedrich was the most famous German conscientious objector. Having refused to serve in 1914 and again when recalled in 1917, he was imprisoned for sabotage. Following release in 1918 Friedrich wrote a book 'War Against War' which was published in 1924. In order to undermine claims of the glories of war his book carried graphic photographs of men with horrendous facial injuries.

Bertha von Suttner and Alfred Hermann Fried inspired the formation of The German Peace Society in 1892. Throughout the war this organisation tried to keep in contact with other peace organisations across the world. This was difficult and in fact they had only limited contact with British pacifists. During the war the organisation was very limited in the extent to which it had any influence.

The League New Fatherland (Bund Neues Vaterland or BNV) came into being in November 1914. While its numbers were never more than 150, which included about 30 from the Peace Society, it contained some of the best minds in Germany at the time. These included Albert Einstein, Kurt Eisner, Hellmuth von Gerlach and Otto LehmannRussbult. The purpose of the mission was to change German foreign policy through change in the political structures of the country.

It was not until towards the end of the war that the pacifist voice was heard in Germany. By this time the soldiers at the front were showing signs of dissatisfaction with the direction the war was taking. The civil population too began to be disillusioned with the war and pacifism began to make sense to them also.

Welcoming Refugees

With the German occupation of Belgium on August 4th 1914 many Belgians left their homes in search of safety from the invaders. Their fear of violence was justified and more than 5,500 civilians were killed, many victims of mass executions by German troops. It was not long before many Belgians started to arrive in Britain. The Government decided that these refugees should receive the same help that British citizens would be entitled to. Initially reception centres were established in London but the numbers arriving were so great that they were immediately dispersed to Liverpool, Manchester and Glasgow.

About 19,000 refugees came to Glasgow and they were dispersed around many towns in west and central Scotland. Local families, hostels, hotels and grand houses all provided shelter for these unfortunate people. The towns and cities of the east coast were unable to accept refugees. The reason for this was the fear that their proximity to the North Sea made them vulnerable to invasion. Foreign nationals living in the east might facilitate German invaders. As a result the authorities decided that no aliens should be located in that part of the country. Consequently, such towns as Aberdeen, Dundee and Edinburgh raised funds to support the west and central towns to provide accommodation. Businesses and churches of all denominations also raised funds for the cause.

Many of the men were skilled workers with trades and professions. Women tended to enter domestic service. While there were slightly more men than women there were also many children. Ages ranged from 1 to 86 with over 2,000 children and those of school age were soon being provided with education.

By and large the Belgians were welcomed and housing was made available and Trades Unions ensured that employment was provided at the same rate as locals. In 1916 newspapers were prohibited from making adverse reports about Belgians or referring to them as aliens. This is because there tended to be widespread suspicion of foreigners. Belgians, however, were seen as victims and so there was widespread sympathy for them. Belgian men fought in the armed services and King Albert I, who was in control of the Belgian Government in exile, agreed to compulsory conscription of men aged be-tween 18 and 41. This mirrored the legislation for British men.

As soon as the war was over repatriation took place. This was largely voluntary and by April 1919 only 480 remained. Most of these too soon left and very few decided to remain in Scotland. This was no reflection on the reception they had received. Indeed many received both British and Belgian awards for their outstanding service to the refugees.

Life on the Home Front

As one would expect, the War had a considerable impact on everyone who stayed at home. Some of the pressures that were created on society were surprising. The historian Clive Emsley points out that with many potential criminals being enlisted in the armed forces there was a decrease in crime. On the other hand, during the 1914 – 1918 war, with women taking on many of the occupations previously in the domain of men, children were thought to be rather neglected, especially when it came to discipline. In addition, boys lacked good role models in their fathers, teachers and others who would have influenced their behaviour. Another factor was the 35% of Scottish policemen who joined the armed services; this caused a crisis in policing in Scotland. Not only was there a shortage of men but the policemen who were left tended to be older men. The Secretary for Scotland told Chief Constables that in order to 'fill the gap' in numbers both 'Additional Constables' and 'Special Constables' were to be employed. The additional constables would be paid and employed only for the duration of the war. Special Constables were not paid and expected to see their volunteering as a contribution to the war effort. This strategy worked well with hundreds of men joining up in the first few months. Many who joined had military experience while others were 'notable' men in the community. Amongst the willing recruits were those who were clearly unsuitable like the busy Selkirk G.P. Dr. J. S. Muir. He served a large area as a doctor and was over 70 years of age. The majority, however, were younger men, many in their 30s.

There were numerous regulations under the Defence of the Realm Act passed in August 1914 (known as DORA). DORA's impact was mainly on the lighting restrictions but extended powers gave government the authority to censor the press, ration food, and restrict the opening hours of public houses. Anti -War demonstrators could be imprisoned and ordinary folk could be tried by court martial. Many of these laws were resented and the special constables who enforced them were resented too. People complained that they were not proper policemen, though high ranking officers saw their presence as invaluable.

In addition to DORA legislation was passed that required enemy aliens of military age to be interned or repatriated. There was a great deal of anti-German feeling at the time and riots occurred in some places with Germans living throughout the UK feeling intimidated because of their nationality. Even the Royal Family who bore the name Saxe-Coburg-Gotha (in German Sachsen-Coburg und Gotha) felt it wise to change it to Windsor. There was a widespread fear of German spies. In a court case where a man accused another of being a German spy, the Procurator Fiscal said, "to be called a German spy was at present time one of the worst terms that could be applied to any man."

The Aliens Restriction Act of 1914 was passed by Parliament. Germans who lived and worked in Scotland in that year found themselves being called back to Germany for military service. They did not always want to go because they had made a new life for themselves in Scotland but they had no choice. In August 1914 the Hawick Express reported that one man who was forced to return to Germany shouted to his colleagues as he left, "Now see that some of you fellows shoot that damned Emperor of ours before you are done"! In October 1915 it was reported that, apart from those who were repatriated, 32,000 were interned.

The civilian population did not escape the war. As we have seen women found themselves being recruited into industry making armaments and doing much of the work that had previously been done by men. Shortage of farm labour resulted in children staying off school in order to help with the harvest. The authorities were far from pleased with this but in the end a week's holiday in October became an established part of the academic calendar and was soon dubbed "The Tattie Holidays".

Many men in the reserved occupations resented having to stay at home while others had to go off and fight. One example of this was Mr. Forsyth, head teacher of Kettle Primary School. In January 1916, having been accepted by Scottish Board of Selection in Cupar, he requested permission from the School Board to enlist in the armed forces immediately. This was denied but the following month a teacher on his staff, William Couston (28) was called up. The 36 year old head teacher pursued his desire to join the armed forces and this eventually took place on 30th October 1916. Clearly the desire to become part of the British fighting force was very strong and, no doubt, was fuelled by propaganda in the local and national press. Letters from the front and pictures of the injured being transported by hospital trains kept the general population informed about what was going on at the front.

Women at home knitted socks for the troops and parcels were put together containing such things as packs of cards and sets of draughts, dominoes and Ludo. The important thing for the troops was to know they were not forgotten. In these days, before the National Health Service, it was necessary for fund raising to take place to support the local hospitals and medical services. Lady Cochrane of Cults did valuable work in ensuring that the local medical services were properly funded. In 1917 lighting restrictions were imposed and blackout was in use in such public buildings as schools. With food rationing in 1918, life for those at home was getting increasingly hard.

William Couston (Left) with his brothers Robert (Centre) and Tommy. William was a teacher at Kettle School

Transport

Vital to the war effort at home was the movement of men, machinery, weapons and food. The railways were the most efficient means of transport at that time and so they came under the authority of the Railway Executive at the outbreak of war.

In February 1917 the Euston to Thurso passenger service came into operation. It was the longest passenger service in the country and existed to connect the Royal Naval bases at Scapa Flow, Invergordon and Rosyth with the remainder of the country. Demand for transportation from the north of Scotland to London followed the demands of the Navy and so this was an irregular service which took much pressure off the regular services.

It became known as the Jellico Express after Admiral John Jellico who constituted the Grand Fleet in Scapa Flow in 1914. Only Naval personnel were allowed to use the service and discipline on board was the responsibility of a senior Royal Navy Officer. The number of passengers varied considerably but on average there were about 300. The Officers were provided with sleeping compartments while the ordinary ratings had to make do with normal carriages. Every carriage had a corridor and some compartments had bars on their windows and were used to house prisoners. With a 717 mile journey it was necessary to make provision for refreshments. Those leaving Euston Station received tea before departure and a bag containing a supper was provided for the journey. A stop was then made at Inverness for breakfast at the Station Hotel. Travelling south tea was provided at Inverness and at Kingussie the Officers dinners were delivered to the train. Clearly there was strict division between the 'Officer Class' and the rest!

Most of the rail network found itself severely stretched with a shortage of personnel, many having joined the forces, and a shortage of locomotives because many were shipped overseas. This resulted in limiting services to what was required. Holiday specials and cheap fairs were abolished and dining and sleeping cars removed from many trains. Nevertheless passenger numbers remained high throughout the period of the war.

With the high casualty rate during the war it was necessary to transport many injured and ill men to hospital. For this special Ambulance trains were brought into service. They provided a bed for those who required it and specialist medical services on board.

With the heavy demand for ammunition it became necessary to establish a cordite factory and this was sited at Gretna. Up to

800 tons were produced in a week at its peak and 11,500 women and 5,100 men were employed to produce it. This put a heavy demand on the railway to transport the workers to the site and the finished product to its markets.

Factories for the production of munitions began to appear throughout the country and this further increased the role of the railways in the war effort.

With 186,000 railwaymen leaving their jobs to fight in the forces (10% never returned) it was necessary to recruit women. Wives were often required to help their husbands and were poorly paid if, indeed, remunerated at all! Soon women were being employed in most of the jobs that the men had done. There was union opposition in many cases but the need for personnel to keep the trains running overcame their reservations.

The importance of the rail network in the First World War cannot be overstated. The men and women who served their country on the railways were keeping the country moving and ensuring that people and weapons, food and workers could all be where they were needed, when they were needed.

The Home Front in Germany

Germany suffered similar problems as Britain including the lack of manpower. Incomes were drastically cut and women found it hard to provide for their families with husbands at war and having to rely on meagre government allowances.

As in Britain women filled the role of men in the workplace but they always felt inferior to their fellow male employees working beside them as well as the men who were fighting in the war. It had been made clear to many by their employers that once the war was over their jobs would be given back to the returning men resulting in the women becoming unemployed. Teachers were conscripted into the army and so it was necessary for young people to leave school earlier than they would have intended to. Many of these youngsters found employment in the arms factories giving them financial independence for the first time.

The lack of food in Germany was a major problem. What food that was available was too expensive for most families. As a result, sickness and death increased through malnutrition and disease. While food laws were introduced in order to ensure fair distribution, poor decision making by the authorities made this less effective that it should have been.

Zeppelins

The war was taken to the doorsteps of the civilian population for the first time mainly through Zeppelin air raids. Eastern England and particularly London had been subject to bombing raids since 1914. With a range of about 1,000 miles these craft could not travel more than 500 miles from their base. This put much of Scotland at the edge of the range that they could attempt. All of this meant that there was no expectation of a raid and the arrival of the L 14 that night in April 1916 came as a big surprise. There should have been gun defences and fighter planes in place but there were none. The cities in the south received warning of air raids by the electric power being dropped twice before being shut off. So the public found their lights dimmed and then they were in darkness. Blackout was enforced. But there was no blackout in Edinburgh. Of course, most households relied upon gas lighting. People were encouraged to cover their windows with blankets to prevent the escape of light and this was enforced.

Edinburgh and Leith were easy targets for the German attackers. The port at Leith, which in 1916 was a separate authority from Edinburgh, had been made aware of the presence of the Zeppelin because Wireless communication between the airships and their base had been monitored. Fearful of a false alarm, the information was withheld from Edinburgh's emergency services. As it happened there was a major fire at Bertram's the engineering company early in the evening. That blaze might have attracted the Zeppelin's crew, though this incident was over long before the raid started at 11.30 pm.

The first explosion was in the dock at Leith. The casualties were two rowing boats and skylights on two Danish sailing craft. Next was a raid on Commercial Street which killed a 66-year-old man and a fire was started at a neighbouring property. A lady who survived the incident reported that she saw a bomb fall through her ceiling and on through her floor to the flat below, which was vacant. She poured water through the hole in the floor successfully putting out the fire that was started by the bomb. The Sandport area was next where two families with eight children between them had a narrow escape. On across the Water of Leith and four bombs were dropped on Leith Hospital and the Manse of St Thomas's Church. The three occupants of the house, minister, his wife and servant, all escaped but the house was destroyed by fire. It is believed that the intended location was Hawthorn's Shipyard that was next door to the hospital.

The L14's most dramatic hit was a fire started at a bonded warehouse on Ronaldson's Wharf. There are stories of local people helping themselves to the whisky that was, they said, 'flowing in the streets'. A baby was killed near Bonnington Mill where the iron works had probably been the target. While much damage to property took place at Leith there were only two fatalities. Once over the city of Edinburgh the L14 dropped an incendiary device which failed to ignite near Edinburgh castle. The next target was the Royal Infirmary, but there were no injuries and little damage. One David Kirkwood was visiting a friend in Morningside that night and recorded in his autobiography "My Life in Revolt" that it was after midnight when he saw a great flash from the Castle. Above him there was the terrible noise of the Zeppelin's engines. When Morningside Asylum was hit the patients panicked and there was much shouting to be heard. Then he witnessed two bombs explode over Leith, one starting a fire. Colinton was the L14's next target and then on to Slateford where it dropped its last bomb before heading out to the North Sea.

Tragically some were killed or injured that night and there was some damage to property, yet April 1916 lasted long in the memory of Edinburgh folk. Many questions were asked about the absence of blackout and lack of preparedness of the city to protect itself against such an attack. On the other hand Edinburgh, unlike many of the English cities, was not a prime target for the Germans. Rosyth Dockyard was the real target but the airship lost its way.

Later in 1916 the responsibility for defence against air raids passed to the Royal Flying Corps. With the establishment of an airfield at Edinburgh the city was given the protection it sought should another air raid take place. This airfield was known as Turnhouse Aerodrome and is now Edinburgh Airport. The police reaction to the fear of air raids was to become obsessed with the regulations about lights. Some were so officious that the Home Office was moved to point out to the Police that prosecuting people for striking a match at the seaside or in the open was unnecessary. Edinburgh was not alone in fearing the Zeppelins. Lighting restrictions included the headlights on cars and any breach of the regulations brought heavy penalties. In Jedburgh

Sheriff Court several convictions led to a fine of £15.00 or 21 days in prison.

Zeppelins brought the violence of the front to the doorstep of the civilian population. While the primary aim was to find industrial and military targets, inevitably civilian casualties took place. While the number of Zeppelin raids over Britain as a whole decreased after 1916, by the end of the war about 1400 people had been killed with 700 of them in London.

French Postcards

Fred Mitchell, grandfather of my wife Ann, sent postcards home that had been embroidered in the villages of France. Long strips of fabric, usually silk, organdie or muslin provided the background upon which the patterns were embroidered. The designs were repeated again and again on the strip of cloth. It was then taken to a factory where it was cut into rectangles and mounted on cardboard before a decorative cardboard frame was glued on top. These were very popular because it allowed the soldier to communicate messages of hope and cheer with his loved ones at home. Letters could become difficult to write for the experiences of the soldiers were neither hopeful nor cheerful. Many of the designs were floral with forget-me-nots, roses, red Flanders poppies and the pansies being the most popular. Religious themes were included at Christmas and Easter. The heads of war leaders, regimental badges and medals were also popular. Below we have an example of a Christmas card and one from the Royal Army Medical Corps Medical Corps which bears the flags of Britain, France, Belgium, Russia, Russian Czar and Italy.

Both cards were written to Fred's young niece Madge. The messages are affectionate and cheerful, not at all reflecting the reality of life as an ambulance driver.

Another C.O. who became an ambulance driver was James, or Jimie, Fleming who sent cards to his girlfriend, Lizzie Young. Mostly they were expressions of love. There is no mention of what is happening at the Front. Behind the lace envelope on the card below was a small card with a simple message: "From Jimie", clearly no more needed to be said. In time Jimie and Lizzie were married.

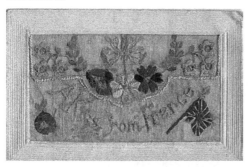

German Postcards
In 1918 a German soldier named Asmus sent the following post-cards home:

"Dear sister and children, In God be praised – I am healthy and well and hope the same for you. How my dear Mini writes. Muller from E. has died in the war; poor Christine with the little children. I pray that God will grant that the evil war will soon be finished. This card is a sight from hay harvesting. Best wishes and be with God. Yours Asmus."

"Dear Thea
For your dear letter my heartfelt thanks. I have been glad that you
can write already and I hope that you will help your mother with her
work. Couldn't Claus write a letter? Is Metha very brave? Greetings
to aunt Mini when she stays with you. Greetings to all of you.
Asmus" (Claus is husband of his sister and was fighting in the east)

If there is one message that comes across clearly in all of the letters and post cards sent from the trenches it is, "I love you dearly – please do not forget me for I may not return!"

CHAPTER 5

Let's be Parochial!

Many men returned from the war both in Europe and beyond. It can be forgotten that among those who fought, a number had to confront the Turks in Mesopotamia rather than the Germans and Austro Hungarians in Europe.

Above we see photographs of some of those who returned. Amongst them was George Fergusson who is standing in the photograph with an unknown friend who is seated. On the right, George is at home with his wife Christina. Below, George, back row, second from the right, can be seen with his comrades in the Middle East.

Sometime after the war, possibly the late 1920s or early 1930s there was a pageant in Ladybank where some of those who returned featured on the float.

While not everyone can be identified we find amongst them familiar faces:

Seated on the far right is Sandy Campbell, next to him George

Fergusson. Standing behind them is Mr. Updahl the Ladybank baker. On the far left local joiner Dave Thomson is leaning against the

piano. While I have not been able to identify the others, perhaps you can.

George Fergusson's Medals

Through the period of the War folks at home had the constant worry of loved ones whose lives were in danger. There was also the pain of grief when a loved one was taken. Isabella Duncan recorded the death of her younger son in October 1918. James, the elder brother, survived the war but died in 1932 aged 36.

James Duncan (seated) and his
Younger Brother William

**In Loving Memory of
WILLIAM DUNCAN**

*Who was lost on the mail boat 'Leinster' sailing between Kingstown
and Holyhead on his way home from Curragh Camp,
10th October, 1918.*

'In my Father's house are many mansions'
*The golden sun was sinking in the west,
The labourer's toil was over for the day,
A soldier's wife stood by her cottage door.
And called her little children in from play,*

*The frugal supper past, with eager face
They gather round that gentle mother's chair
That consecrated spot beloved by God,
Made sacred by the children's simple prayer,*

And kneeling there, hands folded on their breast,
Their faces turned to Christ, the children's friend,
(Who loves their praise) they lisp their evening
prayer,
This night when I lie down right to the end,

Oh God bless mammy and my daddy too,
And all my friends wherever they may be,
And when the war is over, blessed God,
Bring daddy safely home to mother and to me,

The mother kissed her dear ones both good-night,
And laid them in their little bed to rest;
But as she turned to resume her work.
Bring daddy safely home found echo in her breast,

Away in Curragh Camp, across the Irish Sea,
A little band of Highlanders together sit,
They spend the night in mirth and merry chat,
And help their pal to pack his humble kit,

For he was going home; ere very long
He'd see again the bonnie hills of Fife,
Where his old folks await to welcome him,
His little bairnies and his faithful wife,

Wild blew the gale on that October morn
As to the 'Leinster' hundreds took their way
Not wind or storm can daunt our laddie's heart,
For he's got leave and going home today

But ere the 'Leinster' many knots had sailed.
What brings that horror to the Captain's face,
A submarine, 'Oh God preserve us all,
Our only hope is in Thy saving grace.'

The women wept, the children shrieked aloud,
But tears or cries wont stay the murderer's hand,
A torpedo is fired, the 'Leinster's struck,
The Captain turned to make again for land.

Too late. The murderer's work is not complete,
The noble Captain's efforts are in vain,
Another shot is fired, the 'Leinster's sunk
Beneath the cruel waves, no more to rise again,

And one who listened to the bairnies' prayer,
Sent to this earth a messenger of love,
He saw their daddy's spirit hovering there,
And bore him safely to God's home above,

Thy will be done, Great God, not ours the choice,
We fain would keep the ones that you would take,
But though we mourn, we will not complain,
Thou knowest best, Thou makest no mistake.

Fain would we clasp again that loving hand,
Fain would we hear that cheery voice once more
But grieve we not as those who have no hope,
Our dear one is not lost, but only gone before,

Only a little while we too shall hear the call,
A few more years, our summons too will come
And we will go where our dear boy stands
To welcome us to God's eternal home.

Written by Isabella Dunn Duncan, 1861-1932
On the death of her son William

CHAPTER 6

Lambs to the Slaughter!

I t is often said that those who fought in The Great War had little to say about their experiences. This is entirely understandable because how could they give adequate expression of what they had gone through to those who had not been there? Occasionally we get a glimpse into their world, but it is only a glimpse. The unfinished letter of Second Lieutenant Alfred Horace Martindale of the Royal Sussex Regiment gives us just such a glimpse:

"My dear Mother and Father, I got my parcel to-day. I was in despair about baccy and the 2oz. has just tided over the crisis. The butter will be useful too-it is always a treat to have home-made butter. I forget where I was when I last wrote but I believe billeted in a school house.

Well, after three nights there we started off at an unearthly hour and marched to a place we were told was our destination. Having arrived there, we were ordered seven miles further to a delightful village where our Coy. Officer had a jolly farm house allotted to us for a billet. We had just got our kit off when we were ordered to proceed four miles further so we set out again. When we had gone about three miles we were ordered back to the last village, so we had our farm house after all. It was marvellously clean with a nice old garden, neat and full of pears and walnuts. The village was all mellow brick, wonderfully peaceful. Next day we started off again in motor lorries, very soon passing through country of which I know every inch. We passed a mile or two beyond this and were dumped in a muddy field. Here we spent two nights. Imagine yourself suddenly dumped in a ploughed field and made to stay there 48 hours with the rain falling piteously all the time. For beds we had nothing but pools of water but really I don't think I am the worse for it. Then one night we (our Coy.) were suddenly shot into an advanced trench. For two days I had nothing to eat but a pound of biscuits. I made no attempt to sleep and I was drenched through several times. The way up to this trench was through another, two miles long- this took six hours to get up and in the latter part our men, utterly exhausted, were sleeping side by side with men who would never wake. One night I had occasion to walk right across the battle field alone by moon light. It was an appalling sight. During the two days we were attacked twice with bombs and when we came out......"

There the letter ended. This description of the conditions these men endured illustrates the lack of regard the army had for the welfare of its soldiers. Being ordered to march further than necessary, sleeping in the most appalling conditions and the lack of food were all common complaints. It says a lot about the character of these men that they endured so much with a stoic resolve.

A friend of Lieutenant Martindale was able to tell his parents how he died in the following letter: *"A.H. Martindale was at the Cadet School with me and was gazetted to the K.O.Y.L.I (Kings Own Yorkshire Light Infantry) on the same day. He was killed on October*

4 in an unsuccessful attack delivered by two companies on the Hohenzollern Redoubt near Bethune. His company was the second over the parapet. The leading company was practically wiped out by machine gun fire. Only half of the second had followed them when the attack was stopped. Martindale's platoon sergeant was with him all the time and returned with the news of his death. I don't know whether the Hohenzollern Redoubt is yet in our hands but when it is taken I suppose Martindale's body will be recovered and confirmation of his death sent to the War Office. Meanwhile I'm afraid there is no doubt he was killed. In two days we lost six officers, all jolly good fellows."

While this must have been a dreadfully sad letter for Alfred's family to receive, at least they discovered what happened to him. Many, many families never learned how their loved ones died

Lieutenant Alfred Horace Martindale

Fife's First V.C.

Sergeant David Finlay V.C.

David Finlay was born in Guardbridge, Fife on January 25th 1893 to Mr & Mrs George Finlay. He was one of eleven children and his father, a farm worker, frequently moved from farm to farm. As a result, David attended schools at Forgan, Gauldry and Balmullo. When he left school he started to work as a ploughman but his heart was not in farming and in 1910 he joined the army. By 9th May 1915 Dave had risen to the rank of Lance Corporal. It was on that day that the 2nd Battalion of the Black Watch was engaged in the Battle of Aubers Ridge. The aim of the attack was to break through the German line north of Arras. The Germans were well prepared with machine guns while the British and Indian soldiers engaged in the battle had little effective artillery support. Not only had they to face enemy fire but also negotiate a ditch which was wide and filled with water. Previous attempts to move forward had been defeated by this ditch and, although bridges were built they soon disappeared.

David led a bombing party that attacked the enemy lines. At one point he was knocked unconscious when under fire. Once sufficiently recovered he realised that ten men in the group had been badly injured, two of them died. Lance Corporal Finlay then ordered two of the survivors to crawl back to safety while he carried an injured comrade about 100 yards back to a safe position while under fire. For this act of bravery young David Finlay received the Victoria Cross. This battle resulted in a slaughter of historic proportions. There were 12,000 British and Indian casualties. Of the 450 soldiers of the 2nd Battalion Black Watch that were engaged in the battle, there were 276 casualties.

By the time David received his medal from the King he had been promoted to Sergeant. The Dundee Courier tells us that on 30th July 1915 forty decorations had been presented at Buckingham Palace but only one V.C. Afterwards David said that the King spoke very kindly to him, but he did not tell the nature of the conversation. Nor did he elaborate on the act of bravery that earned him the country's highest honour for valour. Indeed he is presented in the newspapers as a quiet, modest man.

Guardbridge had organised a public subscription and presented the hero with a purse of sovereigns. At David's request the presentation took place quietly in his grandmother's home. On July 27th he was married to Chrissie Cunningham. They had known one another since David was sixteen. On the day of his wedding David cycled from Letham to Glenfarg to see friends and then on to Cupar for his wedding at 3.00pm. Back at Glenfarg, a large crowd had gathered to wish their hero and his wife well. Being a very modest man David had to be persuaded to take part in the celebration.

Having been granted just one week's leave to receive the medal and get married, it was a very busy week for David. He rejoined his battalion in France before being posted to Iraq. Sadly David would never return to his new wife and his home in Scotland

Sergeant Finlay was sent to Mesopotamia. Turkey had entered the war on the German side on October 29th 1914. During a battle against the Turks on 22d – 23rd November 1915 when more that 4,000 British and Indian troops were killed or wounded, the remainder of the 8,500 men were forced to take refuge in the town of Kut-al-Amara. There they were surrounded by the Turks who laid siege on them. Lasting 147 days this was to be the longest siege British forces ever had to endure.

January 21st 1916 was a period of heavy rain and was known as 'the flooding season' in the part of Mesopotamia (Iraq) to which David was posted. He found himself one of the 4,000 troops of the 7th Division advancing through No Man's Land deep in 600 yards of floodwater in the first battle of Hanna. About 60% of the British force was killed or injured and no ground was gained that day. David was one of those who died in a bayonet charge across open flooded ground against established trenches with multiple machine gun emplacements. It was January 21st 1916, four days before his 24th birthday. There seems to be some confusion about what happened to his remains. Some say his body was never found while others report that he was buried alongside many Black Watch men in a graveyard in Basra.

Sergeant Finlay is remembered on the war memorials at Moonzie and Leuchars. His V.C. can be seen in the Black Watch Museum in Perth and his name is recorded in the Roll of Honour. David Finlay was the first Fifer to receive the Victoria Cross in World War One and the second Fife V.C. to die in action

For most conspicuous bravery and devotion to duty on 9th May 1915 near Rue de Bois when he led a bombing party of twelve men with the greatest gallantry in the attack until ten of them had fallen. Lance Corporal Findlay then ordered the two survivors to crawl back and he himself went to the assistance of a wounded man and carried him over a distance of one hundred yards of fire swept ground quite regardless of his own personal safety.

Andrew Garland (left) with brothers David (centre) and John(right)

Sapper Andrew K. Garland 410272 Royal Engineers

It was not uncommon for brothers to find themselves all serving in the armed forces. Pitlessie's local joiner, Andrew Garland, together with his older brother David and younger brother John, joined up to serve their country. We are fortunate in that Andrew kept a diary covering his service in the Royal Engineers from January 1st 1917 until December 31st 1918. This gives us the following unique insight into the daily life of a young soldier during these terrible times.

Monday 1st January 1917 was cold and showery in Rouen and Andrew was fully employed in his trade as a joiner, making doors. Being in the Royal Engineers he had to be adaptable and ready to do whatever was required and often this did not involve being a journeyman joiner. So it was that on the following day he was at the Petit Quevilly Prison Camp while Wednesday saw him back to joiner's duties shafting picks. On Thursday he returned to the Prison Camp marking foundations. Sunday was a working day although he did have time to attend a religious service in S.C.A.

On Tuesday 2nd he received the Cults Parish Christmas Gift, a reminder of home in a foreign land. One piece of excitement on the first Sunday of 1917 was searching for escaped Austrian POWs, but once they were found it was back to the daily routine, sometimes using his skills as a joiner and sometimes doing more mundane work like cleaning hangers. He said this was very hard work with small rations. Being in the engineers seems to have meant that he could be used for any work including loading timber on to railway wagons or constructing a road in the Prison Camp. Occasionally he was chosen to guard wounded German prisoners.

Conditions could be harsh in that cold winter of 1917, with water pipes freezing and the men unable to wash. On more than one occasion he records washing on the main road 'in a biscuit tin'. On the lighter side, the YMCA hut provided meals and entertainment and there were football matches and cinema.

On Wednesday 28th February he was warned that he was going up to the front and he left the base for Rive Gauche Station at midnight. He journeyed in an old wooden carriage where he made tea and slept on the floor travelling all day and night before joining his company. On arrival at the front line and wearing a steel helmet as protection against the heavy shelling Andrew had the mundane task of digging a two foot deep trench for the latrines. It is difficult to imagine but in the midst of all this, recreation did take place. There were always football matches, which the engineers seemed invariably to win, and a concert given by The Balmorals of the 51st Division.

On the 26th of March Andrew saw the German lines 2 Km away and they were told the 'big push' was coming. Next day he was shelled as he entered a shelter. It was raining and the trench was knee deep in mud. He described it as, 'an awful mess'. In the morning the damaged trenches had to be repaired while the shelling continued. On the last day of March he witnessed a terrible fire and saw an explosion on the German front line following a raid by the sixty sixth Royal Highlanders. He recorded sixteen casualties. Then the British Ammunition dump exploded. So the saga continued with shelling being received daily and this followed by necessary repairs to the trenches, often involving the heavy work of shovelling mud. The weather was cold, sometimes with rain, often with snow. At times food was scarce and they were frequently bombarded by gas shells.

Monday 9th March, "Barrage fire all night, boys go over at 4.30 am. We watch artillery duels all day. Germans over the ridge by midday. Artillery move to advanced position during the afternoon and night. Reported heavy losses in our Division. Saw captured German Staff. One of our balloons breaks loose but the men on board escape by parachute." Hydrogen filled observation balloons were commonly used by both sides for gaining intelligence on the activities of the enemy. The flammable gas that filled the envelope made them vulnerable when attacked and the observers frequently had to use parachutes to escape.

Inevitably young Andrew saw dead Germans lying in the snow, and he was often under machine gun fire. Then it was back to filling sand bags, washing wagons and guarding prisoners. On 22nd April he was hit by a piece of shrapnel. Although able to walk to the dressing station, it was necessary for him to receive treatment in hospital. While there he was expected to help clean the ward and its windows. On May first, Andrew was discharged and declared fit for duty.

By now the weather was warm and he was able to have some relaxation, though once more there were various tasks that had to be done including painting wagon wheels and making a table for the Officers Mess. The death of comrades was frequent and always recorded. By summer filling in shell holes seemed to be the main activity for a while until he found he had arrived at an 'Old German Dump' in "No-man's-land" and once again under fire.

In June the weather was hot and tiring. Andrew was billeted only one mile from Ypres. "Allemande" (it's interesting that he reverts to the French word for 'German') shelling of Ypres continued the whole day and for the next few days the only escape from the dugout was to search for drinking water. The battle raged with the 'screams' of artillery fire filling the air all day. A nearby railway and dump was shelled and a British plane hit by shrapnel and forced to land (safely behind British lines). In the midst of all this Andrew was busy making notice boards and a butcher's bench. The irony of performing these everyday tasks surrounded by such death and devastation is hard to escape. He tells us that German bombing raids get 'a hot reception' but usually got clear away. Air raids and shelling were, by now, a daily occurrence. Young Andrew found the dead lying everywhere, in shell holes and in trenches. Repairing trenches remained an important task. Clearly this young man was not being spared any of the horrors of World War I.

Throughout this difficult time there were few pleasures but those noted seem to include the occasional, much needed bath. Life in the trenches was such that there was little opportunity to maintain any sort of standard of personal hygiene and so disease was widespread. Another pleasure was receiving parcels sent by Miss Nairn of Rankeilour and, of course, pay day which occurred on Fridays.

Andrew tells us that several men were gassed during heavy shelling on Saturday 14th June. The next day, he reported sick and was sent to the hospital by motor ambulance having been diagnosed with 'Trench Fever'. This disease which affected about one third of British troops who reported sick was transmitted by lice, reflecting the unhygienic conditions under which the troops had to live. Andrew remained in bed in hospital all day. When he left the hospital he was transported on a train dedicated for the use of 'gas cases' and he added, "of which there were not a few". After a long journey he arrived at Le Havre and boarded a ship named the 'Aberdonian' which took him to Southampton. There he transferred to a train for Edinburgh arriving there at midnight. Andrew was admitted to the Edinburgh Royal Infirmary where he remained until August 20th. Then it was off to Kelso for convalescence before he finally returned to Pitlessie on Friday 31st August. Andrew had survived the Third Battle of Ypres which continued until the fall of the village of Passchendaele on November 6th.

While in Pitlessie Andrew went to the pictures in Ladybank, and to Dundee where he visited the family of a friend he left in France. His uncle Harry took him rabbit shooting and he had tea with the minister at the manse. Church attendance was important to Andrew and he seems to have taken every opportunity to worship God throughout the two years of his diary. It is not surprising then to discover that he took the opportunity to attend church at Cults while at home.

Andrew was required to return to duty on September 10th when he was sent to Kilwinning and given light tasks which included sawing firewood. While there he had the opportunity to go to Glasgow for a Rangers-Celtic match where Rangers won 2-1 and also a Cup Final where Rangers beat Partick Thistle 4-1. Then it was on to Staines castle to practice 'barbed wire entanglements'. Andrew and his comrades became expert in this skill and travelled around Scotland demonstrating to troops in Cromarty and Aberdeen.

Being considered fit for duty, he left for France on April 1st 1918, arriving at Le Havre on Wednesday 3rd, then back to Rouen. Soon he found himself digging trenches and 'wiring' in Forceville on the Somme. It wasn't long before Forceville came under enemy fire and one member of the wiring party was killed and seven injured on the first day. At this time food was in short supply, the canteen at times being unable to supply anything. On Thursday 2nd May Andrew and nine others were gassed. Two days later Forceville was again shelled and an Escort of Borderers near his billet were all killed.

Andrew was required to work in several sites on the Somme at this time. He was transported in trestle wagons to such places as Acheux, Mailly-Maillet and Louvencourt. There he was required to dig out old trenches and lay barbed wire entanglements. At this time he said rations were decent with only four men to a loaf. A few days later after laying wires while under enemy fire, there was nothing to eat when they got back to the canteen.

May 1918 was difficult for Andrew and his comrades as they were constantly under fire as they continued with their tasks of repairing trenches and laying wire entanglements. Gas forced them to retreat from their billet and one of their number was killed while laying the wire. Incendiary devices known as 'Golden Rain' were dropped from planes at night. Casualties continued as their work progressed while under attack by 'Fritz'. Day after day he was kept busy laying wires, digging out trenches, repairing damaged shelters, laying tapes marking an extension to the minefield, building a shelter for the 'Yanks' who had arrived; finding themselves under fire, seeing comrades killed and injured. Conditions were terrible with mud everywhere in the showery weather. On one occasion he was considered too untidy for guard duty, on another he had to get a tooth extracted. Illness struck several times and he had to report to the M.O. Searching for wood for the canteen was a constant job and, with food in short supply, they went scrounging for apples.

As the summer advanced so the number of casualties increased and, at times, Andrew was forced to stop work laying wire because they were under fire. Then on August 16th he fell ill, having been gassed and attending the M.O. was necessary. This resulted in a return to Rouen and hospital. He was allowed only 11 days for treatment before he was back digging trenches. This did not last and he was soon put on to lighter duties so clearly he was not yet fit for heavy work.

The men were finding this a difficult time. Andrew recalls a significant incident the evening of September 6th though the details are unclear. He tells us that a Staff Commander spoke to Canadians in D.H... Then, "The place gets rushed. We are lectured to by S.O. on parade". Then, he says, seven hundred men from the base march on Trouville and "smashed the guard" on their return.

Andrew's condition seems to have been deteriorating for when the M.O. tried to mark him fit he was marked B instead. He also found he was not 'officially employed' and so he seems to have kept himself busy by attending a French class at the YMCA, lying on the grass enjoying the sun and reading. A few days later he was declared 'Officially Employed' again. By the beginning of October he was declared fit, though he seems to have continued do light duties for a time, being posted to Rive Gauche on the 11th. Soon he was back in the thick of the battlefield at Monchaux. There he was engaged in building and repairing bridges. At one point, he once again landed in no-man's-land running out tape to a bridge.

As November arrived so did the rain soaking everyone and, on one occasion, coming through the roof of their billet. On the 11th Andrew began to hear rumours of an armistice being signed at 11 am., otherwise life continued as before until he had to report to the M.O. with boils and was consequently given light duties. This seems to have involved working in the billet and stables. The Church service the following Sunday was one of Thanksgiving because the War had ended, but this made little difference to the life of this Sapper. Tending the horses and digging latrines continued to be the daily chore. At times food continued to be in short supply and hunger noted in the diary. On the other hand the opportunity to go to the cinema and theatre with his friends became a more frequent occurrence and on one occasion he said the dinner was good!

Sapper Andrew K. Garland's final entry on Tuesday 31st December 1918 reads,

"All quiet (On The Western Front)."

Alexander MacDonald

While many survived engagement with the enemy at the front, the poor conditions, mustard gas and irregular diet may well have contributed to later illness. A Cupar man, Private Alexander MacDonald, died of peritonitis less than three weeks after his marriage to Annie Simpson in Edinburgh on March 27th 1917.

Alexander was a piper, one of a band of very brave men. For centuries the pipes had been used to convey to the troops the emerging strategies as the battle developed. By the First World War the role was to inspire the troops. This they did by being the first to be 'over the top' playing a rousing tune like "All the Blue Bonnets Over the Border". They carried no armaments but led the attack under heavy gunfire playing all the way. Casualties were heavy with around 1,000 losing their lives. The bravery of these men was well rewarded with decorations including the V.C. being granted to many.

Alexander was such a man. He lost a lower leg in battle and was subsequently awarded the D.C.M. The citation read: "For conspicuous gallantry. He played his pipes through the first and second enemy trenches and when the bombers advanced to the third trench, he continued playing at their head, his companion piper was killed beside him at point blank range."

Alexander was the sixth child of Robert and Mary MacDonald who were married at Kemback on December 10th 1881 and had a family of 10 sons and three daughters.

Born at Falkland Wood on November 14th 1890 he joined the Black Watch Battalion when they were posted to France in 1915.

Funeral of Piper McDonald D.C.M. January 1917

He returned to Fife after being discharged because of injury and subsequently married Annie, who was from Buckhaven. The couple were married in a civil service at 34 Chambers Street Edinburgh, but then tragedy struck when Alexander was admitted to Adamson Hospital, Cupar and died on April 16 1917 following surgery for appendicitis. The Black Watch was in attendance for his funeral and, although he did not die of war injuries, the Commonwealth War Graves Commission erected a memorial plaque in at Cupar Cemetery.

Subsequently his widow moved to New Zealand although it is not known whether she stayed or returned to Fife.

Alexander's parents endured great sadness during their lives. As well as losing Alexander, three other sons were killed in action during the Great War.

Mary died of influenza at the age of 54 just days after her 19 year old son James was killed in France while her husband, Robert, died of stomach cancer in 1916, aged 55.

Robert Niven,

A young man who survived his World War One experiences and went on to live a full life was Robert Niven of Kilwhannel Farm, Ballantrae, Ayrshire. Robert was to become father of Ladybank resident Jane Buchanan.

Twenty year old Robert joined the Ayrshire Yeomanry in 1914. Each new recruit received a printed notice from the Adjutant instructing him to provide himself with:

1 pair of strong and serviceable boots; 1 pair of braces; 2 pairs of drawers; 2 flannel shirts; 1 piece of soap; 3 towels; small canvas bag containing: 1 pair laces, 1 toothbrush, 1 razor, 1 shaving brush, 1 comb, 1 knife, 1 fork, 1 spoon, 1 'housewife' containing needles and thread.

A.I.Y. Sports Musical Ride
Arranged by Sergeant Mavor & L.V. Popkis
Annsmuir Camp, Ladybank

Thus provided he was transferred to Annsmuir near Ladybank for training and home defence. Life at Annsmuir was what the individual made of it. Drills, Brigade mounted drill and Brigade field days. The days were filled with activity. There was also time to relax and football was popular, other activities included the Brigade Cross-Country competition. A cricket team played against local clubs and curling was popular in winter. The local golf course was well patronised and a shooting syndicate enjoyed the sport at Ramornie Estate. There was a regimental farmyard with 100 hens, 30 pigs and an unspecified number of pea fowl.

Communications between the Brigadier and his men were, at times, difficult. He just could not understand their accent. On one occasion when he was inspecting the stables he saw something lying in a corner and asked what it was. "Only a clout in a poke, sir" was the reply. The Brigadier left, none the wiser.

Concerts and sporting events were part of life for the Yeomanry at Annsmuir and all well reported by the local press. So, when, in September 1915 the Regiment was obliged to leave Ladybank for the last time, the locals were sorry to see them go and came out in large numbers to wish them well. The train left at 11.15 am starting a 19 hour journey to Devonport.

Many years later Robert's daughter Jane married Howe of Fife farmer James Buchanan. Jane is, of course, the source of this interesting account of the wartime experiences of her father. I shall let her continue the story in her own words

A Coincidence
Robert Niven (1894 – 1972) was born in Ballantrae, South Ayrshirc. In 1915 along with other farmers' sons and country boys he joined the Ayrshire Yeomanry part of the Lowland Mounted Brigade, and was sent up to Annsmuir Camp for the summer months. For all country boys it was expected they would excel at horsemanship but, alas, that was not to be as horses, in their minds, were used for farm work. So, only a week or so into their time at Annsmuir, they were issued with bicycles and that was how they had to traverse the heather. Robert's two sisters came up from Ballantrae to Ladybank by train for a day visit and to say "goodbye" to their brother.

On 11.15am on 26 September 1915 they set out from Ladybank Station via Edinburgh, Carlisle and Preston for Plymouth en route to Gallipoli. They boarded the Arcadian and set sail from Devonport, escorted by two destroyers, making their way towards the Azores; it was reported there were submarines in the Bay of Biscay. Four days later they passed through the Straits of Gibraltar and on past the coast of Africa arriving in Malta for two days on shore. Then they sailed on through islands near Greece and Crete in the danger zone for submarines, and made it into the harbour at Mudros Lemnos. There they got the news that four ships had been sunk with one only two hours behind the Arcadian.　　On the 11th October they set off in the HMS Partridge, which had been used on the Ardrossan-Belfast route, for Cape Helles.　　Landing in the evening they went straight to the trenches at Rest Camp where they joined French troops already stationed there.　　Next day there was heavy shelling from the Turks in the morning.　In the afternoon the British, together with their French compatriots, returned the fire. This was their lot until the end of the year when Trooper Robert Niven and company were moved on to Egypt.

AYRSHIRE YEOMANRY on
Ladybank south bound platform -
26 September 1915

At first the Division concentrated at Abbassia near Cairo and then in March took over part of the Suez Canal defences until October 1916.　　The following year they were involved in the Second and Third battles of Gaza including the capture of Beersheba and the capture and defence of Jerusalem in December 1917.　　In the early months of 1918 the Division prepared to move to France with embarkation from Alexandria.　By this time Trooper Niven was hospitalised with malaria and dysentery and sent back to the UK for rehabilitation.　He was not demobbed until 3 April 1919.　Then it was back to the farm to resume his quiet way of life.

In the 1930's Robert Niven and his two sisters moved up to a farm north of Perth.   There he married, had two children – one being Jane who married the local farmer, John Buchanan, at Drumtenant.   In 1963, Jane's two aunts visited the family at Drumtenant arriving by train at Ladybank Station.   On walking to the top of the stairs at the station Aunt Jean looked out over the square and pointing to the buildings over on the right said "There used to be a bakers shop over there called Opdahl's – I remember it well".

Jane's aunts had not been in Ladybank since the summer of 1915 – what a memory – what a coincidence.

In the Regimental story of the Ayrshire Yeomanry, "The Proud Trooper" by W. Steel Brownlee, it is recorded that there was a great deal of dissatisfaction with the canteen supplies. A request was submitted to the War Office for a 'Field Force Canteen'. The reply that came back was, "No hope". The Generals at Gallipoli realised that the diet of salty bully beef, hard biscuits, apricot, plum and apple, was not only monotonous but totally unsuitable in such a hot climate. By October it was recorded that half of the 100,000 men on the Peninsula were unfit due to poor diet. When Lord Kitchener visited the area he was pleased to find the Y.M.C.A. was established.   Their stock, however, consisted entirely of nuts. Sometimes troops were able to get some small luxuries from the canteens of visiting ships. On one occasion a riot broke out when the men discovered that the goods they were paying for were labelled, 'A Present From Queensland'!

As we saw in the diary of Andrew Garland and letter of Alfred Martindale, the shortage of food was a matter of major concern wherever the troops were located. While it appears that one hundred years earlier Napoleon was aware that "An army marches on its stomach" the War Office was unaware of the importance of good food for the fighting forces.

Food was not the only hardship when it came to trench warfare. In his book 'Storm of Steer' by Ernst Junger we find the memories of a World War One veteran, vividly recalled. Ernst's experiences may have been that of a German but the British and allied experiences were no different.

Robert Niven (second left) with fellowTroopers near Cairo Egypt 1916

Ernst was a young man experiencing his first engagement in battle. When the artillery started shooting he found it difficult to tell whether it was 'ours or theirs'. As they were advancing they were engaged with French troops. *"Through a stuttering swathe of machine-gun fire, we plunged back into our communication trench, and moved to a position previously held by the French."* There he describes the horror of finding decaying corpses all around. *"In amongst it all"* Ernst tells us, *"were all the bodies of the brave defenders, their guns still poking out through shooting slits."* It was, he said, *"a peculiar feeling, looking into dead, questioning eyes – a shudder that I never quite lost in the course of the war."*

The Devonshire father of Margaret Sproule, of Cults: Frank Rockey

Seventeen year old Frank Rockey enlisted with the British Army at Exeter Barracks in July 1917. There he received his uniform and went with others to Sutton Veny, near Westminster, for training. He was there for about three months with the T.A. before going to No 12 Camp at Salisbury Plain. He was then transferred to the 4th Battalion of the Devonshire regiment and received a further six months training.

On the eve of Saturday 6th April 1918 they were transported by train to Folkestone where they were billeted overnight. Next day Frank and his companions sailed across the English Channel to Boulogne and were then transported by lorry to Etaples. At that point they were transferred to the 1st Battalion Duke of Cornwall's Light Infantry and another train journey taking them to Aire-sur-la-Leys. It was late when they arrived and the only place to sleep was in the station itself. Early next morning it was necessary to march to Thienes to join their Battalion and then up to the Front Line. Their arrival was late at night but the following day the Germans made themselves known by attacking three times. This was Frank's initiation into the war and he and his Battalion stayed there for five days and five nights before being relieved by another Battalion. He had four or five trips to the Front Line before being sent back to Brigade H.Q. on a nine week course on signalling. Then it was back to the Front again.

Frank was engaged in a full day's march to a rest camp where the Battalion stopped for a few days. It was then that, through the cold, wet and unsanitary conditions he fell sick with Trench Foot. Men stood in dirty water for long periods leaving their feet exposed to the danger of infection. If untreated, gangrene could develop and this would result in amputation. He was transferred first to the 1st Australian Clearing Station before moving on to the 24th Stationary Hospital at Etaples. After a few days he was examined by a Medical Board and passed B2. This resulted in him being transferred to Royal Fusiliers (Garrison Company) and so by train to a station only 20 kilometres from the Front Line. After staying under canvas for a couple of days, Frank with a Lance Corporal and another Private had to escort five German Officers to Le Havre by rail.

Once he returned to his Company he was ordered, with others, to go by motor lorry to Mericourt-l'-Abbe. There his job was guarding traffic at a level crossing. Then it was back to H.Q. which had moved to Amiens where he was patrolling from the station at Amiens to St. Roche. He was on then to Ailly-sur-Somme where he had to guard a Ration Dump before going back to H.Q. for demobilisation. Then it was off to Rouen where they marched through the town to another camp. There they had the opportunity to have a bath and a clean! Frank finally arrived back in England when his life in the army ended on February 6th 1919. He finished his account of his life of military service with the words, "Peace, perfect peace".

While the above account is full of facts, it tells us nothing of how Frank felt about his life in the army in World War I. Like so many, he said very little about his experiences though he did write letters. While they say little about what he saw and heard while 'At the Front' his feelings are very clear even when trying to 'put a brave face' on things.

On April 13th 1918 he wrote to his Mother and Father:
"Just a few lines hoping it will find you quite well as it leaves me at present. Sorry to have kept you waiting so long for a letter. I daresay you have been wondering why I have not written. But we have been and had a little experience of what fighting is like in wartime. That's exactly what they told us when we left Salisbury Plain that we were

not going to do. But don't worry we are back for rest now. Well did Fred go away last Saturday week or not? If he did let me have his address. And ask Mrs Buckland for G. I have not seen any of the chaps home there, here yet. Will close now. Goodbye with best love to all from your loving son Frank. Remember me to all in Brischam and home there.
Not much time will write again in a day or two.
If you write to all in Chester let them know where I am as I don't expect I shall have much time for a bit. I hope it will soon be over. We haven't had much sleep lately. Will write again as soon as possible."

Less than two weeks later Frank writes home again:
"Just a few lines hoping it will find you all quite well as it leaves me at present. And to let you know I received your letter on the 24th April and the parcel today the 26th April. I was glad to get the letter saying there was a parcel on the road for we don't get a lot here. Well I sent away a field card on the 24th saying I had your letter hope you got it alright. And I sent a letter and a plain post card 5 or 6 days ago asking you to send some writing paper and envelopes and a parcel. Well I am writing this in the trench behind the front line. Hoping I shall soon be back in England once more. Well we went up in the front line for the first time last Friday week in the night. I shall never forget that night as long as I live, for we had been marching about all that day from early in the morning and when we got to the Front line we had to dig ourselves in. I was tired I can tell you. Well we were in this trench three days and we came out on the Monday night and we had hardly any sleep all that time. I tell you I shall be glad when it's all over the quicker the better. Well how does Fred like Army life let me know when you write and give me his address. Well I must close now so Goodbye with best love to all Father & Mother, Brothers and Sisters from your loving Son.

Frank
XXXXXXX XXXXXXXX XXXXXXXX XXXXXXXX

Remember me to all in Brischam and home there. Will write as often as possible"

On April 30th Frank sounds very low:
"Just a few lines in answer to your letter which I received today dated 24th April. I hope this will find you all quite well as it leaves me at present. Well I wrote the other letter two or three days ago but could not post it as we had to go up the line again, and we can't post any whilst we are up there. I am writing this but not knowing when I shall be able to post it. But I wrote it so as to post it as soon as we go out for rest.

Well if you can send on a parcel every week. Don't send any cigarettes as I get enough to last me, as we get them issued. What we get out here to eat for a day is only enough for a chap's breakfast and we got to make it last all day! You can send on a few pasties if you can get the meat but don't trouble if you don't get very much because you want that for yourself. If you do send any don't put in any onion. I shall not worry so long as it is something to eat. You can put in some envelopes and paper when you send them as we cannot get any here. Well I think Fred looks smart in his uniform already. But I expect he wishes he was home. I know I do. I could not realise what it was like before I came out here. If I get the chance to come home I shall never want to come out here again as long as it goes on like this. I wish I never saw the place. You can get a little rest home there but you are on all day and night time here. If you aint got anything to do, you can't sleep for the blooming shells. Well I must close now so goodbye with best love to Father, Mother, Brothers and sisters, from your loving Son, Frank. [I got 4 shilling order alright before I came over here.]."

Frank's suffering was far greater than is revealed in his letters. He was eventually diagnosed with 'Shell Shock' a condition that remained with him for the rest of his life.

Franks parents had much to fear because Jack Rockey, Frank's elder brother, died in September 1916, probably in the first Battle of the Somme, aged 22. As a result, Frank was keen to reassure them of his love. His need to show affection and to be remembered by friends and relations shows his feeling of vulnerability. We shall see in others the same love and need to be remembered.

Chapter 7

The German Experience

In The Navy.- Our Expedition to Great Yarmouth.

The following letter was written by Franz Brunow-Kosel on board the G. M. Heavy Cruiser "Geydlitz" on November 5th 1914. It describes his feelings as he and his comrades prepare to shell Great Yarmouth.

"It is the afternoon of November 2nd. Three months have passed already and we have seen nothing of the enemy, still haven't measured our strength against them. And yet we have such a burning desire to take revenge for our comrades resting on the cold sea-bed and to exact retribution for those that the war has made cripples. Till now our patience had been severely tested. Already many are complaining, envying comrades fighting on land in Belgium. Why weren't we heading out and attacking the hated British? We couldn't pass judgement, we simply had to wait. Our top brass had to know when the hour would strike for us to put our lives on the line for our beloved fatherland, our hearth and home, our wife and child. And our hour came indeed. It was already being rumoured some days earlier that something special was being planned for us. The nearer we got to our point of departure, the more the excitement grew. Just what would the next few days have in store for us? Each one of us was no doubt asking this question, where are we bound for? We were well aware that we were heading for England, but what part would be our

target? Joyous high-spirits reigned everywhere, a feeling of empowerment arose in every heart, happiness shone in every eye, - well, and what of fear? Can there still be any room at all in one's heart for a feeling called fear? No –

And so the decisive moment when we raised anchor and slowly made our way in line down river. Our comrades on the ships remaining behind envied us and looked at us wistfully. How moved we were as we passed by the Hildebrand and the music, the beloved air, "Deutschland, Deutschland uber alles" was played on board, and in solemn silence the crew wished us a cordial farewell and a successful mission. And our journey continued. Light was slowly fading. In high spirits we reached the open sea. Now the order of the day was: "Ready for action". The enemy was lying in wait for us, in particular the dreadful branch of the service, the invisible submarine. In total blackout the steel bodies of the heavy and light cruisers slid through the deep waters of the North Sea. To a certain degree it was a clear moonlit night. Everyone was at his post, guns loaded with live ammunition. The crew not on watch slept by the guns. Some swopped opinions, others kept to themselves with their thoughts of home and their loved ones. I wonder if they suspected we were heading towards the enemy? Definitely not. Those on the bridge and on the searchlights were on the highest alert. A sharp lookout was being maintained. But nothing was to be seen, no sound broke the profound silence. After we had passed north of Heligoland, we changed course, and headed westwards towards the enemy. Our aim was to arrive at the enemy coast at dawn to give him an unexpected morning greeting from the brass muzzles of our guns.

Tremble, O England, who until now have never seen an enemy on your coastline, now you're going to see what it's like. You who started the war, you who have trampled international law underfoot, now you're going to experience the terrors of war on your own doorstep. And our journey continued. At great speed our sharp keel cut a furrow through the moonlit surface of the sea. And yet, as we travelled in silence through the darkness and were mindful of the coming morning, compassion stole into our hearts. How many innocents had to suffer once more. We imagined the massive panic when our shells fell as a morning greeting on the coffee-tables of the utterly unsuspecting townsfolk. A grim fate, but war knows no pity. Is one showing us any, aren't we being hounded by the entire world!? And on and on it goes towards the enemy, towards an unknown outcome. But fearlessly and faithfully. Disaster may lie in wait for us, because the enemy is also alert, and how easily might one of the treacherously laid mines bring our mission to a premature conclusion. Our light cruisers which had maintained contact on either side during the night, took up position by us at daybreak, two in front, two astern. In this fashion we approached the no longer distant shoreline. Now the order was: "Be doubly alert!" Everyone stood in readiness at his post, cheerfully prepared to lay down his life. Gradually morning dawned. Now we chanced upon a lot of Dutch fishing boats that waved happily to us as they peacefully went about

their business. Further down the coast we ran into English fishing vessels that immediately hoisted their flag, and, on recognising us, raised their hands in horror, unable to warn their homeland of the imminent danger. We continued steadfastly on our way, ripping numerous nets to pieces. What value did an individual's property have for us! We hadn't been spotted by the enemy so far, so we'd crossed without incident. We'd already got within ten sea miles from land, when an enemy light cruiser and a few destroyers came into sight on the port side in front of us. Now the long awaited moment was before us. And then,......the order to open fire. A flash, a single roar and the shells from the brass muzzles were hurtling as a morning greeting towards the enemy. While one section of our ships fired at the speedily retreating enemy, the others launched a salvo at the town which had just come into sight on the coast. I wonder how the inhabitants must have felt. I've no wish to think of it. But how we felt, I can't describe, being allowed after all to be present as the first to attack proud England on its own coastline. This occasion will be irrevocably imprinted in our memories and remain unforgettable into our extreme old age. And then we continued eastwards towards our homeland, where we arrived unscathed the following night.

What we achieved, we don't know, time alone will tell, but one thing we do know, if the fatherland summons us once again, we'll do our duty faithfully, loyal to our oath, and that it might be soon is our fervent wish. However our greatest wish is that God will put a speedy end to this war, silence the weeping, heal the wounds inflicted on us by the war, and let us return unharmed to our father and mother, our wife and child, and our native hearth."

It is interesting when reading Franz Brunow-Kosel's account of this night when the first attack against British soil took place how mixed his feelings are. Clearly, he feels Germany is justified in going to war. It was his understanding that Britain acted illegally, against international law. Britain and the rest of the world were against Germany putting his country in danger. Clearly in Franz's mind Britain was the aggressor. In spite of this he was not without compassion for the poor people of Great Yarmouth who he believed to be in great danger as a result of their intended actions. Interestingly he expresses his disapproval of the British 'treachery' in defending its shoreline with submarines and mines. The Germans hated the British submarines just as much as the allies hated the German U-boats. Isabella Duncan, in her poem marking the death of her son, saw the sailors on the German U-boat as murderers. Perhaps Franz has the same opinion of the British submariners."

Franz could not help thinking about the devastation the guns on the Geydliz might be doing and the lives being lost. He speaks proudly of doing his duty for his country, even if it meant death. In the same way our military men were prepared to lay down their lives for King and country. Each thought that what they were doing was necessary and right. They would agree with the last sentence in Franz's letter, *"our greatest wish is that God will put a speedy end to this war, silence the weeping, heal the wounds inflicted on us by the war, and let us return unharmed to our father and mother, our wife and child, and our native hearth."*

G. M. Heavy Cruiser "Geydlitz" was one of a flotilla of seven German cruisers that attacked the coast of south east England on November 3rd 1914. That attack on Great Yarmouth had no effect because the shells landed on the beach so there was no damage to property and no loss of life. What the attack did do was make the British realise that they had better defend this coastline because Franz's assumption that Britain was ready for the attack was completely wrong. There were no defences perhaps because there had been no attack on British soil for 250 years. In order to address this complacency two 12 pound Naval Guns were loaded on to a train which patrolled the coast from Great Yarmouth to Mundesley for the remainder of the war. In spite of another two attempts by the German Navy to bombard that coast the guns were never fired in anger. The second bombardment on April 25th 1915 was as unsuccessful as the first but on January 14th 1918 a third attack hit its target. Fifty shells landed on the town resulting in four deaths and a lot of damage.

Alone

One young German, Rifleman Kruse-Fleckeby found himself very alone at Christmas 1914. He recorded the experience as follows in January 1915:

"At 3 p.m. on the 24th December I was discharged from the military hospital, and propped up on my walking stick, which the hospital had supplied me with, I set out on foot on my way to our quarters in Dives. Having arrived in our billet, I found it totally deserted; because my company had left for the trenches on the 22nd December and was to be relieved again on the 26th December. I made

myself comfortable in my quarters as far as possible and sat down to send greetings to my loved ones at home. But I found it terribly hard to find the right words and I didn't continue writing as I was too heavy-hearted. My thoughts strayed back home as to how the Christmas celebrations were probably going in my native land, and I thought of the Christmas of the previous year that I was able to spend at the home of my parents-in-law and fiancée and didn't think of having to spend this much-loved festival alone this year and so far away from home. Then I made my way to the regiment's office to see if by chance there was any mail for me: to my immense joy I received the welcome parcel from the women's guild in Kosel and the prayer book from the minister and because of this Christmas Eve turned into a joyous celebration for me after all!"

CHAPTER 8

A Tale of Two Young Soldiers

The two young soldiers in question have so very much in common. Ordinary young men, one aged 23 and the other 24. Both had a very deep Christian faith and loved their homes and their families. Indeed their letters home are full of affection and clearly they were popular for both had many friends. Being young men of integrity they fought in the war because they believed it was the right thing to do. They were doing it for God, for the King and for their loved ones who they believed would be in grave danger if their country was defeated. These young men had so much in common that had they met they could well have become firm friends. In 1914, however, this was impossible because one was German and the other British. Through reading their letters the absurdity of war becomes plain. Propaganda taught that the 'Hun' and the British were evil, depending on which side you were born. In fact, neither Asmus nor Robert was evil. They were likeable, good young men who gave their lives for what each believed was a noble cause. In fact, they gave their lives for – what? We shall let them tell their own stories as far as possible.

Asmus Johannes Witt

Twenty three year old Asmus Johannes Witt worked on the family farm at Taarstedt in northern Schleswig-Holstein. He was called to military service within the first week of the Declaration of War in 1914.

Asmus' letters to his girlfriend Christine, whom he hoped to marry, and his parents, tell how he longed to be home with them, working on the family farm. Asmus was a German and he died over one hundred years ago. Nevertheless, his thoughts and feelings about friendships, war and approaching death transcend time and nationality. His letters to his parents, brothers and sisters, as well as notes in his diary, were often written in the dark, when it was cold and he was hungry and afraid of death. His last letters carry brave words but it is clear that, while ready to do his duty, he was finding it hard to make sense of the war and the battle that was about to herald his own premature demise.

Asmus Johannes Witt

In August 1914 Asmus found himself training in the German army in the Schloss Gottorf in the city of Schleswig, not far from the Danish border. Not only did he keep a diary but he frequently wrote to his family and the letters have been kept.

The first letter is dated 16th December 1914. He writes to the whole family telling them that they would be amazed if they saw him in Gottorf Castle writing to them on a sofa in the grandest of surroundings. He goes on:

"Now, I want to tell you how this happened to me. In the morning I was standing with the other recruits lined up on the Castle Square and we were equally divided into units. Then we went to the stables, which were to be our sleeping quarters. Here there were beds in the stalls; of course they are only boards covering the stone floor.

There are some stoves but they are quite small in the large room. In addition there are three small tables and benches. Nothing else, like a locker, was in the room. It was terribly cold and there were not enough beds for all of the men. The Sergeant asked whether some of us wanted to lodge elsewhere, at our own expense. My fellow countryman Johannes Magnussen from Boholz and I decided to accept this offer and so together we have rented a room with a sofa and table, near the Castle, for 17 Reichsmark per month. For this we also get a cup of coffee in the evening and a cup of tea in the morning and we supply our own bread. Here I live frugally but comfortably and I enjoy my free time in Schleswig.

My sisters, you would not have been able to visit me had I remained in the stable with 70 other soldiers. Now that I am in my apartment you can come. It is located in the Plessenstraße 22. Otherwise still not much of the military life apart from uniforms which have been issued to us. The Sergeant who issued them was just a monster."

19th December 1914
"If you now see me Sunday, please bring my boots, also my woollen vest, knee warmers and gloves. I am unlikely to get a holiday at Christmas but Johannes and I are going get a small Christmas tree with a few lights in our room.

Here in Schleswig many fear an attack by Denmark, but hopefully the good Lord spares us these horrors of the war. I would so much like to return home and it grieves me that I cannot but I look forward to your visit. My good memories of home give a great deal of comfort.

So greetings for all, your Asmus.

My new address is: Musketeer A. j. Witt, Recruit Depot IIE 84, 18 Korporalschaft, Schleswig Castle.

When you come on Sunday please bring the family picture from my album and mother, you can bring me, too, my vest and a bag for the pictures from home.

PS: Tonight I met Johannes Nissen of Brekling who told me that Peter Clinker from Berend who was a student of theology has been killed in the war. The war is horrible. "

Schloss Gottorf

"January 13th 1915

Dear parents, brothers and sisters.

We had bayonet practice and then we were on the parade ground. In between we were just waiting. It's cold in the stables of Gottorf. Either terribly cold or the whole place fills with smoke from the furnace because the flue does not work properly.

I would like to thank you from the bottom of my heart for the beautiful food you gave me. For lunch I ate a piece of your bread and the apple pie which reminds me of home. Today we worked until half past eight in the evening.

Today men departed again from Gottorf. You should just see the military when we come all to-gether. You might almost think that we could beat England alone. What else are you doing? Have you been spreading fertilizer today? Tomorrow we are shooting again and then we shall have free time. I am very hoarse, because we were quite wet from lying on the damp earth. Well, good night!

Best wishes to all of you from your Asmus".

The family Photograph requested: Asmus is seated second left, with his father, mother and nine siblings. Asmus carried this photograph with him when he went into battle.

January 17th 1915

"My Dears

I want to write even a few lines to you even though it's the soldier's bed time. Today I was in town and got a foot cloth to wear under the stockings that are always wet and dirty because in such wet weather our boots leak. Fine and black loafs of bread are rather small here for 40 Pfennig, so two of us share a loaf for our evening meal. When we go to the canteen, it costs 80 Pfennig for a lunch which is too much and tears a hole in the 33 Pfennigs daily wage".

"It will soon be the Emperor's birthday and by then I shall probably be already in the trenches. But time passes, hopefully quickly, up to

the hour when we may return home as the lucky winner of this war. This is what we hope for but do not expect to take place".

January 21st 1915
"Dear parents, brothers and sisters.
Things have changed for me but not in my favour. First, I lost my Sergeant, which is a painful change since I respected him as a superior and as a human being. It made it easier for me to be brave and faithful to do my duty, and also be a brave soldier in the field. But even if it makes it difficult for me, I will go on with courage and boldness for my country and for all of you and for our future existence. I have been assigned to the 4th company until February 11th when, according to the majors from Schleswig, we will be gone. Yesterday I was given a grey uniform. Unfortunately, I got an old one that was stained. It was probably blood stains. I think it's disgusting to have to climb in such a uniform now.
Your Asmus"

"February 5th 1915
Dear Parents, brothers and sisters!
On Monday, we go to the Lockstedter camp and from there into the field of battle. 103 men from our company are going, all voluntarily. Now I ask you again not to worry too much about me. I must do what so many are doing, but also, I am everywhere in God's hands. We are the generation that must fight. And if it is difficult for me to be away from you, so I will fight for what I love.
Your Asmus"

The following is taken from Asmus' diary which began on 6th March 1915 with daily entries until his death on April 24th 1915

11th April 1915
"When the artillery was in position I was on signal duty. Enemy flares can be seen when they attack us or are already in our trench. I must stay alert because the others are sheltering. The trench is deep enough to ensure that when standing up the men are always protected up to the chest. My friend was sitting in order to be fully

covered. But soon I had to get under cover as well because five enemy bullets hit too close to my head. My back was against the wet clay wall and my feet were in the water. I got up once in order to not get stiff from the cold and cramp. But there were no less than five shots close to my head so I decided it would be better if I kept my head down and went back to my old seat. I don't know whether it was just coincidence, or if the Frenchman could see me clearly.

The darkness of the night was usually as bright as day being illuminated by the numerous flares and spotlights. When we were replaced, all feeling in our legs was gone and we were almost unable to walk. We staggered like little children but once our bodies began to warm up the feeling returned. The Dirt from the side of the trench collapsed in places so that we had to kick it aside out of the way".

April 16th 1915
"A few days ago the enemy blew up part of our trench. There was a terrible hole and numerous casualties. In the afternoon the company split into groups and evacuated the trench. When we returned in the early evening, the damage of the explosion was still clear. There was a hole through which a whole barn could disappear. Folded helmets and dismembered body parts of our poor comrades were scattered around. It was horrible".

April 17th 1915
"It was 4.00 0'clock when I got up again. Early today the weather was nice, I found myself making a comparison between the present and last spring. How can we have war on such a beautiful morning? Such spring weather just doesn't like this war.
Oh, I wish I was home again in the beauty and peace and at work on the farm."

April 19th 1915, 6: 00 A.M.
"We eat with the rats and mice from a table, because there are so many that they walk around with us. The lice will follow soon. There is very little sleep. In the end one is so tired that we sleep, even if there is the sound of gunfire. Then you must always be alert and get up.

Some of our comrades find it hard to waken even for a war. Only sounding the alarm makes everyone afraid.
The worst part is the thirst, the water is terribly scarce. Otherwise you could cook up coffee.
The Frenchman leaves us quite alone today. He has enough to do with his trench work. We also improve our shooting ranges and our trench. As soon as the Frenchman disturbs us by artillery fire or mines, we answer with our heavy artillery and that silences them."

The last letter from Asmus to home:
18 APRIL 1915
"My dear, loving parents and siblings!
It should be a quick last farewell to this world, because, the just God of mankind has decreed that my hour has come. The artillery opened the assault three hours ago. Now anxious, heavy hours follow. But be it as it wants, I'll keep my oath of allegiance to the Emperor and Empire in any case and hope that God may have mercy on me.
When you get this letter in your hands I'm probably already redeemed from all suffering and horrors of this ghastly war. I endured it gladly because it had to be, but I was hoping to return to you all. All that is written in my diary is the truth, as are my letters. I've always had courage and I have never regretted going to war. I always trusted my God. If this had not always been the case I should have been at home. Only one thing is not in my letters, not in my diary; great nostalgia, the longing to be with you again; the desire which is sometimes so hard to fight yet does not discourage me.
How beautiful, how infinitely beautiful was the future I had imagined at home. Do not mourn too much for me. Let it comfort you that I've done everything for you.
Now farewell for all."

With this letter was a piece of paper with the fol-lowing lines:"
"Please send the enclosed letter to Christine. My final wish is: you keep a faithful memory of me."

The farewell letter to friend Christine:

APRIL 18, 1915, three o'clock in the afternoon

"My love, dear Christine,

I now send a last farewell word to you, Christine my love, just as I did to my parents and siblings. When you receive this letter you will know my oath of loyalty with death has been sealed.

I send my most sincere thanks for all your love and all you've done for me. How I longed for the hour when I could look in your eyes and you into my eyes and hold your hand and tell you how grateful I am to you. I was hoping to return very healthy, and that from then my dear friend and treasured companion would be sharing all the joys and sorrows of life with me.

Have you, my dear Christine, wanted to be with me? I think that you'd have regretted not one hour. When I stood in the firing line at night when at my post, and also in the day, my thoughts were always at home with you, dear Christine and my dear parents and siblings. How I begged my God, to allow me to return home. How I did dream beautiful pictures of the future. How I wanted to be with you, dear Christine.

Continue believing that we shall be hand-in-hand in the Father's place. Yes, too good to be true. I will not grumble. But I am thankful that my last memory is of such love as ours. I don't know how you did it but your love has lightened the load I have carried.

Grieve not for me, my dear Christine. By God's grace, we will be together once again for ever. I hope that God will give you a new happiness and much love in your life.

Your loving Asmus "

Asmus dies a "hero's death for the Fatherland":

MOULIN, APRIL 24 1915

"Dear Mr Witt, Unfortunately I must tell you the sad news that your son Asmus died a hero's death for the fatherland on April 24 in the morning in most faithful fulfilment of duty for his country. He succumbed to the enemy missile which hit the trenches when he was at his post.

The company shares with you, dear Mr Witt, heartfelt sadness at the loss of your son Asmus. We lose a brave and loving comrade, who we

will always honour in our memory. Your son Asmus rests, with his comrades, in a small cemetery for the brave eighty six at a place of rest north of Moulin. Those Comrades who were affected by the same loss of a good friend have provided for a lasting memory in the best way. Flowers adorn his grave and a lovely stone with an inscription as a memorial for later times. Dear Mr Witt, be assured of the most sincere condolences of the entire 10th company. Should you wish any more information please contact the company.
The personal effects of your son will be sent to you.

Hamrick, Company Commander"

A memorial service was held on May 5, 1915 for Asmus Johannes Witt in his home church in Taarstedt. His parents and siblings received the sermon text presented by the pastor.

Robert Allan

The second young man is twenty four year old Robert Allan, who hailed from Mount Vernon in Glasgow and joined the Highland Light Infantry in November 1914. The following have been taken from letters and postcards.

Robert's first entry is dated 3rd November 1914. He had just arrived at Southampton after a train journey from Glasgow. It was on that day that he first encountered German soldiers who were Prisoners of War and who were marching past him. The following day Robert   boarded a ship but did not know its destination. His spirits were high as he told his parents to *"keep up your hearts – you should just see how our fellows marched through Southampton today – as if they were going to a ball"*. Being unsure whether he was heading for France or Egypt he told his parents it was difficult to predict when he would be able to write again.

Next day Robert was able to report that he was in France, but orders prohibited divulging his location. Indeed he seems to have been unable to say very much at all about what was happening. He was very keen to reassure his family that he was comfortable and well. His letters are also, like Asmus letters, very affectionate towards his parents and siblings. Another post card to his sister Maisie talks about looking forward to going to the theatre with her when he gets home. He anticipates wearing his *'Evening togs'* for the occasion, though he says, *"I can hardly imagine myself in them and neither could you if you could see me at times."* This was on November 11th, less than a week since his arrival in France. Already he seems to be finding the conditions unpleasant.

Over the next few days Robert was moved to another location. While he does not say it explicitly it would appear they marched to the new position for he complained about having sore heels and he had very little to eat and described it as a *'starvation expedition'*. Trouble with his heels became a frequent complaint as the months passed. Most of the time he considers himself well fed. The diet consisted mainly of tinned beef, which he enjoyed and tinned jam which he described as, *'very good'*. One thing he found strange was that the closer he got to *'Kaiser Bill and his gang'* the less he felt he knew of the progress of the war. Indeed he said he was better informed in Glasgow than he was in France.

The following day Robert said that he found the local people very friendly and, he says British money is 'valid at full face value'. He is clearly concerned for his family, especially his mother, who has been worrying about him and he says, *"it is my earnest prayer to God that in his Providence he will spare you all undue anxiety on my account – if this is so I should feel ever so much more easy – remember what 'Hector' used to quote, "God is in his Heaven – all's well with the world" and whatever the outcome of this business may be I believe it shall all be for the best. I trust that God will spare us all to enjoy each other's company in health and strength for many years, when we shall see things in their proper light and where at the fireside no censor can erase what we desire to say."* As with Asmus, Robert's faith was very important to him and he frequently refers to it in his letters.

Robert was not at 'the front' at this time and the weather was beautiful. Home, however, was so very important to him and his fellow soldiers for he says, *"I am safe in saying there is not a soul in the regiment who does not entertain a higher opinion of home now."* All of this is so much like the sentiments of Asmus

On November 13th Robert wrote a long letter in which he answered several questions his mother had put to him about how well he was being looked after. This gives us some idea of the conditions he was enduring at that time. The food was very adequate with ham, bread and cheese being served for breakfast. Bully Beef (minced corned beef mixed with gelatine) was a staple of the British Army field rations from the time of the Boer War up to 1939. Robert seemed to enjoy it though he did not always get potatoes which he missed. Bread jam and cheese were served up for tea along with any bully beef left over from the mid-day meal which was referred to as dinner. Traditionally for Scottish working class families dinner was always a mid-day meal. Robert asked his mother to please not send any more clothes because he has to carry them in his pack and it gets very heavy. This is another often repeated message. It would appear his mother was very generous with the frequent parcels of food and clothes that were sent out. What he did want was *'1-shilling worth of Cadbury's plain chocolate (not any more) to be sent every Friday.'* On another occasion he said his company had been out marching in the rain and got soaked through. When they returned they were given a small portion of rum to get them warmed up. Later he tells us he is a 'teetotaller' but there was no word of him declining the rum on that occasion! Once again Robert prays for an end to the war and for there to be peace in Europe.

On the 18th he revealed that the route followed to his position at the time of writing was from Southampton to Le Havre, then via Rouen, Boulogne and Calais. Thence to the position from which he was writing which he was unable to divulge .

Once again Robert expresses his desire for the family to be reunited but a note of doubt enters his letter when he says, *"...if I was just sure of this I would be happier in my mind."* On the other hand he reassures his folk that the men are far from down hearted and depressed and that in fact they are cheerful and in good spirits. By November 18th the weather had turned cold and there was snow on the ground. He tells us "Jimmy Thompson is on guard today and I'm not envious of his job" clearly sentry duty in the snow was no joke.

For the first time he refers to the Germans as "the accursed Germans" saying they are "getting *'bashed now on both frontiers and we hope they will soon be worsted."*

By November 22nd, Robert is missing home cooking, and imagines what the family might be having for dinner. At times he says he has eaten food he would hardly have given to Tory, the dog, and yet he ate it *"with relish"*. As an example he says the previous day was spent marching and trench digging. Robert had run out of bully beef and a chap nearby was eating some he had with him. He broke a piece off and gave it to Robert which he gratefully accepted though the hands of both men were filthy. Dirty hands also remove the ham from the pan and put it in the plates for breakfast. It is eaten, Robert says, *"as if it had just been sterilised."*

Now the weeks are passing one running into another with no real 'Sabbath'. How Robert misses the Sabbath now, though he confesses he did not always value it at home.

The letter of 28th November records Robert's first experience of action and, he tells his parents he has earned a bar to his medal, which he prays he will be spared to wear.

They had a three day march through the ice and snow before arriving at the trenches. The first shells landed before they got there but were wide of the mark. Three hours later they came under artillery fire again and Robert took comfort from the belief that what he was doing was *"for God, King, Country and our own fireside."* The sound of the German shells was, he said, *"more like a lost devil from hell itself than anything I could imagine – they come along with the scream of a heavy express train and when they hit the ground they shake the place for how many yards I don't know."* The trench he was in was only about four feet by five feet and he and another man lay in it for two days. Stray bullets whistled over their heads all night and landed just beyond them. In spite of this Robert slept well under the circumstances. *"But",* he adds, *"The speaking during the engagement was done by the big guns on both sides. We were just between them and could hear the German 'Jack Johnsons' and 'Coal boxes' and what not flying like blazes over our heads and trying to hit our gallant artillery men."* It appears a Jack Johnson was the British nickname for German 15 cm artillery shells. It was named after the U.S. heavyweight boxing champion from 1908 – 1915. A "coal box" was the nickname for a German high shell that was fired from a 5.9 cm howitzer that gives out heavy black smoke. Some authorities believe the two terms are synonymous. *"I think for all we hear about the German's firing many shells our fellows can hold a candle to any German, at least during Thursday and Friday. Our guns go off like a great sudden cough and we could hear their projectiles flying over our trench on their way to the Germans. I hope they smashed up thousands of the wretches. But, Father and Mother, I thank God from the bottom of my heart you did not know what War was in Scotland."* The area of France he was in was rural, one of *"the little gardens of France"* now *"like a land under a curse".* There were deserted farms with the occasional pig or cow hanging around their once familiar farmsteadings. Villages were *"smashed and alone – a haunt for spirits".* *"What the cost of a war must be is unaccountable – motor cars – wagons – guns – ammunition and lives!"*

Robert admits that on this occasion he did not fire a shot, *"although the two companies in the fire trenches lashed away bravely the first night and we had the satisfaction of knowing that the German porkers fell back and the British are advancing."* Robert and his fellows came out of this encounter without any casualties although as the battalion was forming up to leave, a stray bullet injured the first lieutenant, but Robert was not sure of the extent of his injuries. *"Poor chap and he is such a fine fellow too"* commented Robert.

On Sunday 29th Robert had a special treat for he was on Church Parade. With the familiar hymns, 'Oh God of Bethel', 'Jesus lover of my soul' and 'Stand up! Stand up for Jesus' his sprits were raised. On the other hand he said there were many tears amongst the ranks when, in prayer the Chaplain petitioned for the "dear ones at home".

It is in this letter that Robert closes by saying, *"I changed my shirt and 'semmit' (vest) for the first time since leaving home to-day – this is for your private guidance."* Having left home on the 3rd of November and this being the 29th, it says something about the conditions under which they were living. Personal hygiene was a continuing problem for both the British and German troops. There were no baths or showers in the trenches.

On December 2nd he tells his folks that the King (George Vth) *"has arrived and will inspect the men on the next day"*. One thing that is disturbing him is the new regulation that the soldiers are to be restricted to one letter every four days. He feels that writing home is so important that censors should be appointed to read the letters before they go off so relieving Officers of this task. As a result all communication with the folks at home will have to be done through his parents for he will keep that one letter for them. His resentment of this is clear when he wrote, *"I always enjoyed dropping a note to my friends, but I suppose we must let this right be wrestled from us since we are only common soldiers!!"*

In spite of the hardships and dangers Robert is facing he is convinced of the rightness of the cause and says, *"I am glad you allowed me to take a stand on your and my behalf for our King and Country."* Clearly both Godliness and patriotism were important motivators for Robert, just as they were for Asmus.

On December 4th Robert tells his parents that he had the honour of shaking hands with the first private soldier to win the V.C. in the current campaign. He was John Wilson from Edinburgh and he alone took out six Germans, captured their machine gun and returned with it to the British lines.

As Christmas approached Robert received many parcels from friends and family. Clearly he misses them all terribly and he longs to return home. At the church parade the minister, in his prayer for others asked God to touch the enemy's hearts with the fire of His love "or if not that they may be smashed with the iron rod of His wrath." This says more about the feelings of the time than the theology of the minister.

On Christmas day Robert's thoughts were with his family and contemplating the words, "Peace on earth and goodwill to all" while sitting within the sound of gunfire. He, and all the soldiers, had received cards from *"Their Sacred Majesties"* and he sent them on to his parents. Something of the feelings of the time are being expressed here. The enemy is all that is evil while the King and Queen are elevated to sainthood.

With the turn of the year to 1915 there was little cheer. On 31st December Robert was back in the trenches – ditches as he described them for they were standing up to their knees in water. While half the company found itself in the firing trenches the other half, including Robert was in reserve. His trench was covered from the rain and he was able to get out of the water and on to a platform. There the soldiers dried their feet, put on dry socks and settled down to sleep. It was a frosty night but that did not stop Robert from sleeping. At 12.00 o'clock he and twelve men fired a salvo of twelve shots at the Germans in the trenches in front and wished each other a good New Year.

Mud was the problem in the communication trench they were using once relieved of duty. They were held up for over two hours as some men ahead were dug out of the mud. He was almost up to his knees in the sludge which made it exhausting to walk.

Once back at their billets the men settled down for a well earned rest only to be wakened in just a few hours. A new communication trench had to be dug and they were given the job of doing it. It was about 3.00 am before they were finished and then, he said, *"we slept!!!"*

By 9th January Robert was recording that there had been a return to the trenches. Once again mud was a terrible problem. He had been given Orderly Duties at Battalion Headquarters which took him out of the firing line. The others were there for three days. It was unusual for a company to be 72 hours in the trenches, normally it was for a 24 or 48 hour stretch. Two of Robert's fellows were killed, one through an accident the other by a sniper.

Food continued to be sent from home. Ham, tinned soup and home baking are the favourites and they supplement the meagre rations provided. In January a haggis was requested, Robert doesn't say so but clearly the Bard (Robert Burns) would be honoured even in the trenches. Socks were also frequently sent and were always well received.

This young man, like Asmus, was looking at the situation he was in with great calmness and maturity. In January 1915 he told his parents that he had received a letter telling him how anxious they were about him. In reply he wrote, *"I ask both of you to be brave – God has been exceedingly good to us in the past and I thank him and look forward with confidence to the future, 'My times are in Thy hands' and your times are too. Of course you might lose me or I might lose you, but all is in God's hands and His plan is perfect – therefore let us press forward with confidence – do so in God's name and it will greatly help me."* Often it is easier to be in the face of danger and doing something about it than to watch helplessly as a loved one faces peril. This was the situation Robert and his parents had been thrust into. One can only feel for the anxious loved ones at home as their son's life could be taken at any time.

A mischievous sense of humour begins to find its way into Robert's letters as on one occasion he reports that the Germans had delivered about 20,000 lbs of ammunition by 2.00 pm. His comment is, *"Not a bad gift from the Huns to the G.H."* (Glasgow Highlanders) Yet, while he was prepared to refer to the Germans as 'The Hun', 'brutes' or 'Porkers' when they were the impersonal enemy, when faced with them he was much more compassionate. In one letter he tells us, *"I have heard a fair number of German prisoners, boys, were taken and they are said to have stated they were told they were only up against Kitchener's army – only boys – and poor beggars were up against one of the crack regiments."* Clearly there was compassion for these boys who were experiencing the worst this war could throw at them.

On the other hand, Robert had little time for those men at home who were not joining the forces. *"What we need to finish this accursed war is more men and the men at home who don't come out ought to be blackmailed and kept severely in the background. I always look at it like this. Peace has to be bought at any price and Britain has to enjoy the fruits of that peace."*

Once again Robert confesses to his mother that washing rarely takes place. *"I don't think many of our men have changed their underclothing more than twice since they came out here."* He goes on, *"The livestock question is one needing great care in the handling of it – to be quite candid I would not like any of my friends at home to sit next to a Glasgow Highlander in a tram car in their present condition – every man has a very fair stock of - ye ken yersel! But you get used to them and it keeps you warm at night wriggling in your clothes to keep them from congregating too much in one spot!"* Like Asmus he was aware of the Kaiser's 56th birthday, but Robert added, *"I hope his 57th is celebrated in a wooden box and I don't wish anyone any ill!"*

Robert wrote excellent letters and they were often quite long. Of course all letters had to be censored and this annoyed him greatly. There were also, at times, restrictions on the length of the letters. Having said that, they were told they could put anything they liked into them, how they felt about the campaign, complaining about the officers, the only thing they could not do was give their position. The Captain, who was the censor, sometimes complained about poor handwriting. It must have been difficult for the men to write clearly because moments were snatched at odd times and in odd places to write their epistle. The soldier had to use whatever was available as a writing desk and this could be a stone, a bully beef tin or whatever. Nevertheless there was a great need to bridge the distance in miles from their loved ones through letter writing. In these essays Robert expressed, again and again, his great love for his family and great desire to be home again. He tried to give what comfort he could through assuring them that he was well and trying always to sound up-beat and positive about his experiences. Most of all, he expressed his great faith in God and in the mercy of Christ, assuring his folk that in the end, 'all will be well'.

On the other hand it was so vitally important for him to receive letters and parcels from home. Reading about family and friends reminded him that he was still part of their lives and they of his.

In February 1915 Robert reported that there had been an outbreak of diphtheria. This resulted in them being unable to send letters. The men were also isolated during the day. At night, however, they were all out together digging. Robert was infuriated by this stupidity. If they had to be isolated it should have been for 24 hours and not just during the daylight hours.

In the same letter he told his mother that at the moment he was clear of the 'live stock'! A creosote bath and clean underclothes seemed to put the matter right. He explains that when they have a bath they leave their dirty underclothes and put on others. Their underclothes are cleaned and fumigated and made available for the next soldiers to have a bath. Their kilts and the rest of their uniforms were also fumigated but Robert was not sure how long they would be able to stay clear of the lice.

On March fifth Robert notes that it was then four months since he landed in France. He describes it as the longest period in his life because so much has happened and there had also been many weary anxious moments. He confesses that at times he complains about things. On one occasion a friend remarked, *"Never mind Bertie, it's all for the folks at home!"* After that he stopped complaining.

Although Robert's health was normally good, the sore on his foot continued to trouble him. It had clearly become infected. He was relieved from duties for a few days and poultices were applied to draw the infection.

Amongst the many things he missed was porridge and he asked his mother to send out some Quaker Porridge Oats and suitable condensed milk. He described how he made it up in his mess tin and then he and his four friends dug into it. Being aware that at one time he would never have considered sharing his plate with others, in this context it seemed to be entirely natural. It is clear from the way Robert refers to his friends that they are so very important to him and he to them. Perhaps they gave one another the feeling of having a surrogate family, sharing the horrors and giving one another much needed support while away from home.

On one occasion Robert told how he saw some French children playing at being in a battle. They threw clods of earth as shells. He found this strangely amusing as they were within the sound of German rifles and wounded and dying men passed by in ambulances.

Come mid March Robert was in the reserve trenches. They occupied a dug out which was a square area cut into the side of the trench. It was about 8 feet by 8 feet and 3feet 6 inches deep. Here up to six of them had to sleep with their kit on. He described how this involved lying head to toe – with someone's boot in his face. If one turns, all turn. Here he remained for thirteen days. One Sunday they decided to have their own service. The hymns they sang were, 'Abide with me'; 'God our help in ages past'; 'Nearer my God to thee'; 'I to the hills will lift mine eyes' and 'All people that on earth do dwell'. There were two lessons read and it finished with 'A Soldier's Prayer' (possibly Psalm 91) and The Lord's Prayer. Clearly God's help for the courage to face whatever is before them was a powerful motivator when choosing the hymns. These young men did not know if tomorrow would come!

Towards the end of March Robert tells us that he was writing from a trench that was about 200 yards from the German trenches. At night, he said, he could hear them singing, some with good voices. Sadly he goes on to refer to them as brutes but perhaps if one has the job of killing the enemy it is easier to think of them as less than human. Acknowledging that they were young men like him would make the job so much harder.

As time passed Robert began to feel he could apply for a commission and he sought the agreement of his parents to do so. But there were aspects of army life that still irritated him. On one occasion he records that the men were paraded for ceremonial drill. Robert reckoned this was fine at Buckingham Palace but in the middle of a battlefield it was a bit much. The men didn't mind being turned out when it was necessary but for this? - They complained bitterly.

Robert comes across as a principled, compassionate young man who was not given to anger. On one occasion, however, he was clearly very angry. A young friends of the family in Glasgow was reported to have said he did not join the forces because war did not appeal to him. Robert let rip, *"Did it or does it appeal to me? If he had seen what our fellows have, war would appeal to him just as it does to us. It appeals as something hellish and as a thing every man should try to stamp out of life forever. That is the only appeal this war has to men and the more men we have the sooner the thing will be over. But the game is ours, I'm sure of that."*

One night when they were out digging they heard the Germans singing (Robert tells us they were good singers). Some of the men gave them a few rounds of rapid fire and the singing stopped. In reply the Germans turned a machine gun on them, then one shouted over, *"How do you like that?"* As their bullets failed to hit anything that mattered, Robert and their friends didn't mind if they wasted their ammunition.

In the following letter, for reasons that are explained in the text, Robert, being free from the censor, gave a more detailed account of what he had been up to from Christmas until the end of March. I shall let Robert tell this in his own words:

26th March, 1915,
"My dear Father & Mother,
This like my letter of 16th ult. is purely a 'speck' - I am going to try to send this home with Freddie's friend-Jack Bartholomew - who is going home to take a commission in the R.F.A.(Royal Fleet Auxiliary). My letter of 16th inst. was given to a fellow who was a chance starter for home — he had rheumatics or something and he promised to post my letter if he got home. He can't be home yet apparently. Well, in the first place I should say we have been in action from Xmas — we started from Bailleul one night about Xmas and went to Richeborg where we had a pretty rotten time (New Year's Day) - that is where the trenches were so wet - I told you about them in my letters of about that date. We were twice in there - the second set of trenches were much worse than the first but as you will remember I was selected for orderly by Capt. Chalmers - i. e. to do messages at Battalion. Headquarters - a perfectly easy job, but I was not sorry to have it. One looks for the easiest things here! You never saw fellows so dejected like, as our men were and muck from head to heel. One has no idea of the mud unless one sees it and its terribly heavy work walking in it - at this place the communication trenches were fearful - up to the knees almost in nothing but mud. From Richeborg we went to a small place called Assures - just outside Bethune - for a rest of 10 days, from there to Festubert. We were here on the day of the great bombardment - 28th January and were in all

six days and nights in the firing line - I may say breastworks - things like dykes - are used here as trenches , fill with water when about a foot deep.

After our six days we were three days and nights in reserve - just behind the 'line' (we had the great feed of haggis here) and then went down to Gorre. Here as my p.c. would tell you we had our diphtheria cases and our digging. We had to go from Gorre to a distance of about three miles every night for almost three weeks.

We usually started from Gorre about 7 p.m. (with shovels etc) and dug or filled sand bags till about midnight or one o'clock and then marched back to Gorre. I say marched - that is wrong - it was very often a most miserable looking procession - the men were often so done.

The sand bags were used to build a new breast work in front of our lines. It was really pretty dangerous work - we lost two poor fellows and one wounded. The latter had bad luck and I thought he was gone for home but he's back with us again - hard lines - he should have been sent home. From Gorre we went up to the now far famed position at Givenchy. I really forget how long we were up and down from there as a Battalion - our Company were in thrice. The first and second times I was there - the third time I was confined to billet with my sore heel. We had to go to Givenchy along the famous La Bassee Canal. Givenchy was once a very nice village - it is now a heap of bricks - a perfect scene of desolation. From this position we went to Bethune and were there for a long rest, four days I think it was - We then went to Annequin. This village is just behind our lines and although the bullets from the Germans could reach the main road of the village yet to a great extent the natives are still there. This position is to the South of the La Bassee Canal and is the furthest South position held by the British Army. (The French were on our right). We were only in reserve at Annequin. I wrote you about my experience there - about the dug outs etc. From Annequin we went to Bethune last Sunday - about 6 miles. On arrival our Company mounted duties — I was on quarter guard — that is sentry duty - 2 hours on and four hours off. On Monday we left Bethune and came up to this position -Lacourtai. We (i.e. our half Battalion) are here for eight days. One company in for a night and day, then out for the same period and so on till our eight days are up. I may say this is a pretty quiet spot. Our butt of the breastworks during the first day and night did not fire one single shot and I don't think the 'Kites' in the other breastworks fired more than five. Of course we have always to be careful.

You will all have heard of the great advance made at Neuve Chapelle. We were then at Annequin. Well I never heard in my life anything like the bombardment our artillery gave the Germans that day. It commenced at 7.30 a.m. and continued without interruption till 11.30 am. One constant war. I have been under shell fire but nothing like yon and please God I never shall. I don't know, of course if in the course of history such a bombardment had ever been heard before - I have heard that unwounded German prisoners taken that day (10/3/15) were simply petrified. I believe we shelled their trenches to the tune of one shell to every 10 yards of trench. As we were in reserve that day I saw quite a number of our wounded going off in the ambulances and some of our men told me one wagon passed with wounded 2nd H.L. I. men and they were singing 'Rolling Home to Bonnie Scotland'. Of course after a day like the 10th the number of little wooden crosses on our side is always added to, but the above little incident just explains to you how the heart longs for home. Men suffering pain and yet glad to sing at the prospect of getting home for even a little.

Now I must close. God can only know how we long - you at home and me here - to clasp each other in a long embrace - but I always know that I have set out on a good cause and I look forward with Faith in Him who is able to keep us from evil and danger and in His good time we shall all meet again, when we pray Britain shall have fought and won a great and glorious fight. God bless you all and may He keep us under the shadow of His wing. Goodnight, Father and Mother and you, the three wee ones!

Your loving & obedient son,

Robert Allan"

Having been within sound of the big guns since before Christmas they were ready, by April 23rd, for the rest that was due to start the next day. The period away from the trenches was short lived and on May 3rd he was back in the reserve trenches. By the 5th Robert tells us that the men who have spent the winter in the trenches are fed up and long to be relieved.

Robert's last letter home was dated 15th May 1915. He was killed in Action the next day at the Battle of Festubert, one of 16,000 casualties in the Battle which lasted from May 15th until May 27th 1915.

So Robert, like Asmus, was returned to God's eternal home.

Men, not names nor numbers

While Robert, Asmus and others tell us about the lice and the rats, they say little about the fear when "going over the top" to face enemy gunfire in no-man's land. They say little about the bodies of their friends, ripped apart by the blast from shells that shook the ground like an earthquake. There are those who talk of decapitated bodies, of men dying having had their limbs torn off or having been disembowelled by gunfire. Let us make no bones about it, death in war is not clean and noble, it is ugly, agonising and barbaric.

This is not intended to detract from the heroism of those who fought. Indeed it ennobles them for in spite of what was happening they "went over the top". No matter how one feels about war or where one's sympathies lie one cannot but feel humbled before such bravery. Many survived the war, often with terrible physical and mental scars and the memory of "going over the top" remained with them on the day they died.

Ernst Junger, the already quoted First World War German officer and author of the much praised 'Storm of Steel' gave us, perhaps, the most graphic descriptions of the horror these men endured.

At one point he recalled, *"One baby-faced fellow, who was mocked a few days ago by his comrades, and on exercises had wept under the weight of the big munitions boxes, was now loyally carrying his comrades, having picked them up unasked in the crater. Seeing that did for me. I threw myself to the ground, and sobbed hysterically, while my men stood grimly about".*

On another occasion he recalls, *"We retreated to the first of the dugouts, over which the bullets of both sides were soon flying back and forth. It looked as though it had been a base for messengers and bicyclists attached to the artillery. Outside it lay my British soldier, little more than a boy, who had been hit in the temple. He lay there, looking quite relaxed. I forced myself to look closely at him. It wasn't a case of 'you or me' any more. I often thought back on him; and more with the passing of the years. The state, which relieves us of our responsibility, cannot take away our remorse; and we must exercise it. Sorrow, regret, pursued me deep into my dreams."*

Such memories may come from a German soldier in this instance, but they were common for all soldiers whatever side they were on. The ghosts of the dead, their comrades and enemies were to haunt them for the rest of their lives.

CHAPTER 9

April 6 1917

When War broke out in August 1914 it was the intention of the American government to maintain a position of strict neutrality. This was supported by the vast majority of American people. There was, however, a close trading relationship between the U.S. and U.K. with goods and people being transported across the North Atlantic by ships including many of the great liners of the day.

Germany had decided, as part of its war strategy, to isolate the U.K. from all trade in the hope of starving its enemy into submission. The Kaiser's government gave warning that all ships attempting to break the German embargo, whether neutral or not, would be attacked. As a consequence of this several U.S. ships sailing for the U.K. were damaged or sunk by German mines. The first to be attacked was a privately owned American vessel, the 'William P. Frye'. The President, Woodrow Wilson, was outraged and the German government apologised, claiming it was an unfortunate mistake and so U.S. neutrality was maintained.

On the 7th of May 1915 a German U-boat torpedoed the British owned 'Lusitania' just off the coast of Ireland. German justification for this was their claim that the ship was carrying military materials. Whether or not there were munitions on board, there were 1,959 passengers and 1,198 were killed. This number included 128 U.S. citizens. America demanded reparations and Germany promised that in future it would ensure the safety of passengers before sinking an unarmed vessel. Nevertheless, another 27 Ameri cans were killed when an Italian liner was sunk killing 272 passengers. By now American public opinion was turning against Germany.

It was the German announcement in 1917 that it would resume unrestricted warfare within their exclusion zone around the U.K. that caused America to break diplomatic relations. Within a matter of hours, on February 3rd a German U-boat sank the American cargo ship 'Housatonic' off the Isles of Scilly. The crew were warned and allowed to leave the ship in lifeboats and the submarine towed them towards shore. In spite of the fact that there was no loss of life the American reaction was such that the U.S. entry into the war seemed inevitable.

On 22nd February the U.S. Congress passed an arms appropriation bill releasing $250 million to allow the country to prepare for war. Late the following month Germany sank four more ships of the American merchant fleet. On April 2nd the U.S. President called Congress to approve a declaration of war against Germany. Four days later this was given overwhelming approval and so by the end of June 14,000 U.S. troops were in France training for combat. By the end of the war over 2,000,000 U.S. soldiers had served with the allies in Europe and about 50,000 were killed.

On December 6th 1917, a French ship, 'Mont-Blanc', loaded with 3,224 tons of explosives, including guncotton, benzol, TNT and picric acid, bound for Europe collided with a Norwegian vessel in Halifax, Nova Scotia. This resulted in a massive explosion which caused a tsunami like surge about 60 feet above high water level resulting in the death of nearly 2,000 people with 9,000 injured. In addition, 3,000 buildings over an area of 1 square mile were destroyed. This disaster is remembered in Halifax, Nova Scotia on December 6th each year.

It was not long after the declaration of war that families across America found themselves being affected by events.

In the small town of Melrose, Massachusetts, 75 men of the parish of Trinity Episcopal Church were soon drafted or volunteered for service. When news of the first casualty reached the congregation the horror of war was brought into the heart of the Parish.

This was the news that Arthur Gibbons had died in France, on 7th September 1918. Arthur was well known in Melrose having been born there in 1891. Here his education took place in the public schools. Through his active participation in the life of Trinity Parish Church as a member of the choir his name appears on the roll of honour.

Arthur's mother was widowed and when she re-married she moved the family to Southampton, Nova Scotia. As a result, Arthur became involved with the war from its inception in 1914 when Canada declared war in support of the U.K. So it is that he enrolled in the 2nd Canadian Infantry. His brother Chester also joined up and by the time of Arthur's death was invalided in England while his other brother Robert was in a Scots Canadian Regiment and fighting at the front.

Arthur had risen to the rank of Lance Corporal and by the time of his death in 1918 he had already served in the trenches for two years. He had also been wounded at an earlier point in the war and once declared fit returned to the front. On September 7th he was fatally injured and died of his wounds in the Casualty Clearing Station.

Just as in Europe the civilian population was quickly involved in the 'war effort'. Melrose women made bandages for the Red Cross and knitted socks for the men serving so far away. Corn syrup was used to replace sugar which was soon in short supply. People were encouraged to save peach stones that were used in the manufacture of gas masks. Silver paper or tin foil was kept and recycled in the production of armaments. What was known as 'Thrift Stamps' were purchased for 25 cents and saved to be redeemed by the U.S. government when the war ended.

Families in the U.S. suffered the same fears for their loved ones fighting in the trenches as the families of every other soldier around the world. At times tragedy struck with devastating force. Such was the case for Wilson and Helena Young. Wilson was a clerk in a steam shop when his son Harold was born in 1899. At that time they lived in Suffolk, Massachusetts. On December 17th 1917, young Harold went off to enlist in the army and was attached to the Thirty Ninth Infantry, one of America's youngest Regiments having been formed on June 1st 1917. Training took place at Camp Green near Charlotte, North Carolina. The officers and men lived in tents and this being one of the coldest winters on record life for the recruits was hard. The area around the camp site was a sea of sticky mud. The consequence of this is that it was possible to pursue only indoor training. It was not until May 8th 1918 that the Regiment set sail for France and the Thirty Ninth became part of the American Expeditionary Forces.

Over the following months the Regiment took part in several major engagements. On September 28th they were advancing over the crest of hill 212, the highest north of the town of Septsarges. At 7.30 am they reached the field of German machine-gun fire. The Americans found themselves under heavy fire and were forced to remain in a position that was not to their advantage. It was in this incident that nineteen year old sergeant Harold Young died. He was buried near the place he fell.

Sgt Harold O. Young

In spite of the large number of American casualties during the war there were those who returned unscathed. Another Melrose man, Clarence De Mar is such a man. Born in Cincinnati, Ohio in 1888, Clarence hated school yet found a place at the University of Vermont. He trained as a compositor and became passionate about children and education. Clarence won the Boston Marathon in 1911 and after the War he went on to win that event another six times: 1922, 23, 24, 26, 27 and 28. He also won the bronze medal for the marathon in the 1924 Olympic Games. Clarence served his country as a soldier but it is as a Marathon runner that he is remembered.

The first of the 182 Melrose men called to service to be killed in action was Private William C. Boylen.

Bill Boylen, as he was known to his friends, was said to be a quiet, retiring man yet with the determination and drive that won him many friends. He was a graduate of Franklin school in 1913 and was known to be an athlete of some standing showing ability in baseball, American football and hockey. He was also a member of Green Street Baptist church in Melrose. In July 1917 the twenty year old enlisted in the 5th Regiment of Malden and was soon sailing for France. Before long he was injured in action and spent his first winter in Europe in base hospital recovering from wounds. Once seen to be fit for service, Bill was back in the front line. On July 20th 1918 there was a 'big push' to drive the Germans back. It was in this engagement that Private William Boylen lost his life.

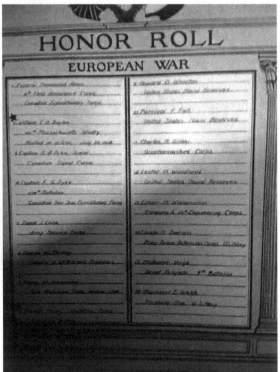

Memorial at Green Street Baptist Church
Melrose Massachusettes
William Boylen and Harold Young are marked with stars

CHAPTER 10

The End of the War

When, in 1917, Russia arranged a treaty with Germany that removed it from the war, Germany felt that it was given an advantage over its enemies. In fact over one million men had to remain in the east in order to enforce the treaty. Yet these men were badly needed in the west to counter the British and allied advance. In addition Russia was in no position to make available the additional food needed in Germany. The war, as well as the Civil War, disrupted Russian agriculture and what was produced they needed at home.

The rise of Communism with its appeal to end the war struck a chord with many. There resulted a wave of strikes which began in Vienna in 1918 and spread to Germany. Nevertheless, German expectations of a successful outcome through an offensive across the Somme battlefields in March were not to be met. At first the German advance was considerable and the British Fifth Army was destroyed. However, the Germans lacked clear objectives and the offensive became a series of limited attacks with no clear goal. In July the French successfully counter-attacked and on August 8th the battle of Amiens started. The allied forces advanced an unprecedented eight miles in one day. While the British suffered 9,000 casualties, 27,000 casualties were inflicted on the Germans. There followed a series of engagements over the next 100 days that led finally to the German surrender.

Germany had lost the initiative and its Austro-Hungarian allies were near to collapse. They were disillusioned with the Kaiser, the military leadership and government. By the end of September German high command informed Keiser Wilhelm II that the war was lost. They wanted Germany to seek an armistice based on peace proposals that American President Woodrow Wilson had suggested.

President Woodrow Wilson's Fourteen Points:
- Open covenants of peace, openly arrived at
- Freedom of the seas
- The removal so far as possible of all economic barriers
- The reduction of national armaments to the lowest point consistent with domestic safety
- Impartial adjustment of all colonial claims
- The evacuation of all Russian territory
- The evacuation and restoration of Belgium
- The liberation of France and return to her of Alsace and Lorraine
- Readjustment of the frontiers of Italy to conform to clearly recognisable lines of nationality
- The peoples of Austria-Hungary should be accorded the freest opportunity of autonomous development
- Evacuation of occupation forces from Romania, Serbia and Montenegro; Serbia should be accorded free and secure access to the sea
- Autonomous development for the non-Turkish peoples of the Ottoman empire; free passage of the Dardanelles to the ships and commerce of all nations
- An independent Poland to be established, with free and secure access to the sea
- A general association of nations to be formed to guarantee to its members political independence and territorial integrity (the genesis of the League of Nations)

The aim of Wilson's 14 points was to achieve a "peace without victory". The first eight points were concerned with territory and political influence. The remaining six points related to ensuring the peace would last and that future wars would be prevented. The final point proposed a 'League of Nations' to act as arbiter of future international disputes.

Versailles

Across Europe Germany was seen widely as the aggressor that caused the war. A meeting of the U.S., Britain, France and Italy ensured that very tough obligations would be demanded of the defeated Germany. So it was that the Treaty of Versailles presented to the German Leaders for their signature on May 7th 1919 made heavy demands. Germany had to lose territories to Belgium, Czechoslovakia, Poland and France. All German colonies became mandated to the League of Nations. The Rhineland was to be demilitarised. With limits put on the German Army, Navy and Air Force, any plans to regain military advantage in Europe were dashed. The most humiliating part of the Treaty was article 231, often called the "War Guilt Clause" forcing Germany to accept complete responsibility for initiating the War. This meant that Germany would be held responsible for all material damage that resulted from the War. Reparations were crippling and Germany was not only defeated but also humiliated.

With the end of the war there was a great sense of relief throughout the world. Perhaps the feelings of the time are best expressed by Hazen Pingree Spinney, an American, whose letter home appeared in the Melrose Free Press in January 1919:

"Dear Mother

It is now one thirty in the afternoon and the war has been over for one hour and a half. I have been busy the last few days, but now I guess it is all over and all we can do is wait.

I have seen some great sights from our hill lately. I saw the final drive taking place and in fact I took part in it. But now it is all over nobody need worry. I have a copy of the official wireless message which we received from German headquarters this A.M., saying that all hostilities would cease at 11.55 a.m. today.

After a rather large evening last evening, today has been a wonderful day. The sun came out and burned off the mist in pretty good shape, so we could see what was going on. The aviators were busy, but along towards 11.45 things got very quiet and have remained so ever since except – It sounded queer to be sitting around taking a sun bath and to remark, "Well five minutes more of war." The bells were ringing in the nearby towns and of course we could not be outdone. So some of us climbed into the tower of the church where the original statue of Joan of Arc stands and for the first time since the war started that bell was rung by human hands instead of by German shells landing near it. Oh it was a grand sound.

So, as I said before, all we can do now is wait and see what we have to do in the line of cleaning up France. So you see, mother, you have nothing more to worry about.

I suppose you people at home have heard the good news and no doubt you are having quite a celebration. Well the French people are having a wonderful time, kissing the U.S. soldiers.

I am going to celebrate by taking a bath, so I will close now. Hoping you are all well and happy.

Love to all, Hazen"

It is not clear why Hazan said that hostilities ceased at 11.55. The fact is that the armistice took place on November 11ᵗʰ at 11 am

CHAPTER 11

PEACE!

All nations paid a terrible price over the four years of military engagement. Following the War, financial hardship was widespread across Europe. In Germany attempts were made to defy the harsher terms of the treaty if they could not be revised.

For the average German this 'peace' that had been agreed brought worry, fear and anxiety. At least the loved ones who had survived returned home, but this peace brought little comfort. There was no ringing of church bells to mark the occasion and certainly no mass jubilation. Fear for the country's economy was widespread as was fear of invasion by the enemy. There was also the fear of political reaction to the ensuing hardship bringing strikes, unemployment and armed uprisings. Following the abdication of the Kaiser on 9th November 1918 and the armistice on November 11th, Germany lacked strong leadership. Civil unrest followed with riots in the large cities. There was widespread concern that Germany would have a full blown revolution and that Communism would take over there as it did in Russia.

Between 1914 and 1918 the German people longed for peace but when it came it failed to bring back the prosperity of the pre-war economy. The extent of the reparations demanded by the allies resulted in the destruction of the German economy. As prices started to rise and shortage of food became widespread so there was the constant threat of plundering, violence and profiteering. It was felt that hard work no longer counted for much. There was the sense that sincerity and honesty had deserted the people and so social cohesion was under threat.

The currency became more and more devalued. To illustrate this there is the often told account of a woman who was carrying her money in a washing basket. She put it on the ground as she entered a shop to make a purchase. When she returned, the basket had been stolen but the money was left behind. Clearly the basket was worth more than its contents!

One German described the peace in the following words:

"Peace has been concluded with Germany at Versailles. However, those to whom this new-born child with the fine-sounding name was so dear, couldn't be genuinely glad of the same, but realised with horror that a changeling had been substituted to them by evil spirits. No bell with exultant ringing carried the news of the conclusion of peace through-out the land. Admittedly the peace had brought home our loved ones (as far as death didn't confine them in his fetters) from the trenches, from the enemy's prison-camps. Nevertheless there is no desire for massive jubilation. Worry about the further development of the state economy refuses to allow it to burst out. The feeling of security is crippled by the threatening entry of the enemy into German territory, by threatening fresh upheaval by the right or left bringing new shockwaves, strikes, endless armed uprisings. Peace! We were hoping for the return of better days from you, such as we knew in the idyllic age before 1914. How you have deceived us! There adheres to you many a rude feature that in no way can be pleasing to us: unemployment and idleness, shortages and rising prices, profiteering, plundering and acts of violence; they have taken on even harsher forms than in the war itself, and sincerity and honesty, hard work and orderliness, they no longer count for all that

much. Peace! If you wish us to praise you, you must show us more pleasant features and reveal yourself to us as the genuine Child of Peace."

Peace in Britain

Before World War One Britain, with its colonies stretching around the world, was economically the superpower of the world. Germany had been spending large sums on armaments since 1912. With the outbreak of War, Britain had to engage in a rapid build up of arms which plunged the country into an economic crisis. The markets had to be reassured and money found to pay for the War. In order to secure the finances taxes were increased and more people found themselves liable to be taxed. Large international loans were secured and War Bonds were sold to the public promising a dividend of 5% and a guarantee to pay the capital back in 1947. With the abandonment of the Gold Standard in 1914 it was now possible to print money and, in spite of its dangers, this is exactly what the government did. By 1932 the 5% return on War Bonds was reduced to 3.5% and the guarantee to repay the capital was rescinded. Indeed that money has never been paid to the investors or those who inherited the Bonds. This suggests that the World War One debt is still with us.

The fact is that economically the country survived the War but found itself in a marked decline. Many countries started to produce goods they once bought from Britain. This not only dried up markets but created competition. With the rise of American influence in European matters and its expanding economy, Britain lost its economic and political influence in the world. This was exacerbated by the loss of Empire.

The inter war years remained hard economically with widespread unemployment and poverty. Just as things started to improve, the country was once again plunged into war. Again debts were created and had to be paid off. As a result, it was not until the 1950s that the British people would begin to see an improvement in the standard of living.

Remembering the Fallen

It is good that Germany, Britain and all our allies remember those who were so brave. With the passage of time the politics behind the event pales into insignificance in the face of the unstinting bravery of all those young men who faced the hellish brutality of war and did not shrink from doing what they firmly believed to be right for God, King, Country and Family. It is important that we never forget them and the evil that led them to suffer and die so horribly.

Across Europe and North Africa the graves of the fallen are tended with care and respect. Throughout Britain and beyond there are war memorials to the dead. In this the Howe of Fife is no different and these memorials can be found in every village and town. By the mid 1920s at street corners and in churches they took various forms.

In Collessie Church there is a brass plate recording the names of the sons of the Parish that failed to return.

Alison Walker who lives in Collessie has researched the men whose names appear on the memorial in the church. This information is contained in a folder that is kept there. Through this we know that Private R. Barclay served in the 43rd Canadian Infantry. He was the son of William and Margaret Barclay of Collessie and died on November 4th 1917 aged 24. Mrs. Barclay had the following inscription put on the stone at Etaples Military

Cemetery. "Until the Day Dawn and The Shadows Flee Away." We also know that George McDonald is buried at the Railway Dugouts Burial Ground (Transport Farm) and that he left all his possessions to his father, George McDonald of Bridge of Earn.

All the men of both the First and Second World War are included and, while the amount of detailed information varies, each one transforms a name into a person, loved greatly, cherished always and missed terribly.

At Giffordtown there is a Celtic cross in the centre of the village

Another Celtic cross stands near the station at Ladybank

A window that once adorned the Free Church in Kettle remembering the dead associated with its members was moved to Kettle Parish Church when the two were united.

A plaque in a wall near both church and Village hall is in a prominent situation in Kettle.

At Pitlessie, outside the Wilkie Hall, an imposing edifice carries the names of the fallen.

Nationally there are memorials in all major cities including Edinburgh, Cardiff and London.

Each year since 1918, at 11 am on the 11th day of the 11th month, the United Kingdom comes to a standstill in memory of those who died. Most people wear a red poppy, reminisent of the poppies of the fields in Flanders.

There are those who see this as a jingoistic act that glorifies war. This is not the case. It is a solemn act of remembrance of the bravery and suffering of those who endured the horrors of that conflict. It also serves as a reminder of the implications and cost of war. The dead of succeeding wars are also remembered on that day.

Memorials in Germany

In Germany World War One has, in many ways, become the forgotten war. It does not unite the people in an act of commemoration the way it does in Britain. Most Germans view the First War as a precursor to the Second and it is difficult for the two conflicts to be separated in the German mind. That is not to say that memorials don't exist, for they do. In Berlin there is the Neuer Garnisionfreidhof cemetery which contains the bodies of 7,200 soldiers who died in World War One. Most were men who had suffered severe injury at the front and brought back to Berlin for hospital care. While many gravestones carry a name and age, some are marked "unbekannte", unknown.

These graves are tended with great care, but few Germans visit them. Britons travel many miles across Europe to visit war graves, but not Germans. World War I did not take place in Germany but in other lands, so it seems to be somewhat remote.

A significant memorial stands in Garnisionfreidhof cemetery carrying a message that may well explain why Germans see the war so differently. It is of a dead body on a podium, covered by a flag. On top are a broken sword and a helmet. Appearing from one part of the flag is the soldier's clenched fist being held into the air. Underneath is the inscription, "Wir staben, auf dass Deutschland lebe, so lasset uns leben in euch" – "We died that Germany lives, so let us live in you." In other words those living are to justify the sacrifice of the dead. Many Germans felt this very strongly in the inter-war years. It is impossible not to see that it had a strong bearing on the events that developed in the 1930s and 40s.

Not all memorials carry such a message. In Niederau in Saxony a memorial can be found bearing the inscription "Through Suffering to Light".

At Pang near Rosenheim, Bavaria the memorial shows the Angel of Mercy which appeared on so many war memorials around the world. Clearly this symbol of God's love and compassion was strictly neutral in this, and in all wars.

In Conclusion

Myths, lies and ineptitude seem to have been the cause of this War. The bravery of all the soldiers who took part was immense. So who were these heroes? They were just ordinary people from all walks of life. Most joined up because they believed it was necessary to serve King and Country – it was the right thing to do. There were also some who saw the services as an opportunity to escape from some aspect of their lives that they found to be unpalatable. Whoever they were, they were amongst the greatest heroes of the 20th century because, in the end, whichever side they were on, they were prepared to "go over the top" to die so that those they loved might be safe and prosper.

The Kaiser abdicated on November 9th 1918 and went into exile in Huis Droon, a mansion house and large estate near Utrecht. There he died in 1941 and in the year 2000 his body still lay in state in the mausoleum in the grounds of Huis Droon. In the year 2,000 the Netherlands Government asked Germany to repatriate the Kaiser's body and some of his possessions but Berlin refused.

*"**They shall not be forgotten**."*

Bibliography & Further Reading

A Scottish Railway Preservation Society Publication. (n.d.).
From Scotland to the Somme.

Asmus Johannas Witt. (15 November 2014). *Schleswiger Nachrichten*, 8.

Bayer, M. (n.d.). 1917 - A German Perspective. *Centenary News*.

Britanica, E. (n.d.). World War I - Killed Wounded and Missing.

Brooks, M. (n.d.). Conscientious Objectors in the Own Words. *Imperial War Museums, www.iwm.org.uk.*

Carr, V. S. (n.d.). Dos Passos: A Life.

Cavell Nurses Trust. (n.d.). Edith Cavell.

Czyzyk, C. (n.d.). Five Inspirational Stories of Women in the First World War. *Imperial War Museum, https://www.iwm.org.uk.*

Dr Sundari Anitha, Professor Ruth Pearson. (2013). Striking Women and Work in World War One: 1914-1918. *Striking Women: South Asian Workers.*

Dundee Courier. (1915, July 13). Patents of Fife V.C. Hero. *The British Newspaper Archive.*

Encyclopedia Britannica. (n.d.). *www.britannica.com.*

Evening Express. (5th August 1915). *Aberdeen Journals.*

Exemptions from Military Service in WW1. (n.d.). *My Learning.*

Jeffen John From The War Chronicle of Kofel Kirchfpiels.

Four First World War Composers Who Defined the Conflict. (21st August 2018). *The Telegraph*.

Hannah Dent, S. M. (n.d.). World War One Medical Evacuation. *FOAR2000 module, Leeds University Library Special Collections.*

Junger, E. (n.d.). *Storm of Steel.* Penguin Books.

Kennedy, M. (n.d.). Forst World War's Forgotten Chinese Labour Corps To Get Recognition At Last. *The Guardian*.

Kitchen, M. (n.d.). Life on the Home Front During the First World War. *www.bbc.co.uk/history/worldwars/Wwone/war_end01.shtml*.

Kitchen, M. (n.d.). The Ending of World War One, and the Legacy of Peace. *BBC History*.

Mason, A. (n.d.). Women in the First World War.

Mullay, S. (2017, January). Zepplins Over Edinburgh Part 2. *History Scotland Volume 17, No. 1*, pp. 32 - 37.

Mullay, S. (n.d.). Zepplins Over Edinburgh Part 1. *History Scotland Vol. 16 No. 6*, pp. 16 - 21.

Ruediger, S. (n.d.). Jerome K. Jerome the Man. *The Jerome K. Jerome Society*.

Shaw, A. H. (n.d.). Is There Any Scandal? A Brief History of the People of the Howe of Fife Parish Church.

Smale, D. D. (2018, January). The First World War and Policing in the Scottish Borders. *History Scotland*, pp. 32 - 39.

Walker, A. (n.d.). Collessie Church War Memorial Tablet.

World War 1. (n.d.). *Holocaust Encyclopedia, www.ushmm.org/wic/*.

INDEX

Lightning Source UK Ltd.
Milton Keynes UK
UKHW02f0759210918
329243UK00001B/1/P